GODS AND HEROES
IN NORTH WALES

GODS AND HEROES IN NORTH WALES

A MYTHOLOGICAL GUIDE

by

Michael Senior

Gwasg Carreg Gwalch

ISBN: 0-86381-249-X

Map: Ken Lloyd Gruffydd

First published in 1993 by Gwasg Carreg Gwalch,
Llanrwst

Printed in Wales

Contents

Author's Note

Parts of the material in this book are based on passages in my book 'Myths of Britain', which was published by Orbis Publishing Ltd and by Book Club Associates in 1979, and is at present out of print. Some of the matter however results from first-hand discoveries I have made in the meantime, in the course of researches for my several local history booklets, all published by Gwasg Carreg Gwalch. In particular there are some new, and I think important discoveries which appear here in print for the first time.

Michael Senior

The author Michael Senior is an international authority on authentic mythology, as well as being well-known as a writer on the history and topology of North Wales. In addition to his many local history booklets, his national and international publications include GREECE AND ITS MYTHS, published by Victor Gollancz, MYTHS OF BRITAIN (Orbis and Book Club Associates), and WHO'S WHO IN MYTHOLOGY, a summary of worldwide myth (published in Britain by Orbis and in the U.S. by Macmillan), which has been translated into several European languages.

Early Britain and its Myths

The myths of Britain form a distinct and identifiable body. What makes them myths is their strong element of symbolic significance. Without this they might better be called legends or folk-tales. With it they have enduring power and fascination. What makes them British is that they are precisely located, just as much as the myths of Greece; and some of them are located in North Wales.

Like all mythology the body of authentic tradition which is the mythology of our country has dual origins. It comes partly from the residue of old religion — myth is in fact partly what religion becomes when it is superceded. It comes also from what one might term proto-history: the hazy memory of real but (in terms of the social development of a people) very early events. These are rather like childhood experiences, which you partially remember first-hand, but know much better from photographs in the family album.

North Wales is fortunate, as we shall see, in having in its area excellent examples of both these types of myth, and of myths which combine the two elements in close harmony. It may help to introduce the subject matter of this book, and to explain what is meant here by 'myth', and hence what will be included and what left out, if I outline here the sort of features characteristic of these two contributory streams of myth — the streams from early history and from old religion.

The aspect of myth which stems from history is not historical in the sense of being a chronological record of events. Myth sees in terms of apparently single and identifiable events things which may have taken a long and often indefinable period to occur. This is not to suggest that such accounts should be rejected as simply fictional or false. They are symbolically or emblematically true. In one North Wales myth the Roman occupation occurs as a single episode, whereas of course it was a long-drawn-out and complex process. To criticise this story as historically incorrect would be to misunderstand its purpose. Its validity is as a symbolic representation.

Another feature of the element of proto-history in myth is very similar in effect. Events of a type which may have happened again and again in different places over a long period are told of, in story form, as having happened once. For instance, the memories of many floods in parts of Europe and the Middle East become represented by the idea of one great flood. North Wales too has its inundation myth, behind which lies a long succession of coastal change.

The religious strand in the origin of myth has, I think, several elements too. It operates in much the same manner as the other: it sets out to construct a mythic approach to things which, again, in some sense happened. But these are not the type of things which happen historically. Rather, being built into the structure of human life, they happen always and inevitably, like birth and death.

The universal, unavoidable, and constantly repeated, have always been seen, ironically, as problematic. An older generation feels its position threatened by a new; a wife whose husband has become more interested in his job than in her, looks for a young lover; the certain knowledge of eventual death confronts them all; continuity persists in the endless cycles of the seasons, the species, and the stars. Myth sets itself the daunting task of making sense of it all.

All these types and themes are represented here. It is as if the subtle but distinct land-form of North Wales attracted the equally mysterious speculations of the human mind. I cannot emphasise too strongly that this is not a book of folk-tales and legends. Myth differs from those in that it is a serious and deep attempt to grasp and express some important truth. This book will deal too with this significance, in the case of the North Wales myths.

It might be of interest, before we tell the stories, to consider where they came from. In literal terms, we can identify from the actual manuscripts which we have the skeletons of earlier records, and may infer behind even those the original oral tradition. For instance, though a lot of important items of early tradition are collected in a document written in about 1100, we can identify the sources from which this was copied as having themselves been composed at various dates back to the seventh century. Some of the crucial historical poetry only exists in thirteenth century versions, but seems to have been first written down at least as early as the ninth, and we can feel reasonably confident that some of it would have been created as oral art at the time to which its contents refer, the late sixth century.

The Welsh work known as the Mabinogion is found in its first complete form in the late fourteenth or early fifteenth century collection known as the Red Book of Hergest, but since bits of it appear in two books dating back to nearer 1300, and small fragments even appear a century before that, we can assume a much earlier original source. Source-dating is certainly a technical and rather controversial matter, but some things are fairly certain. The first of the succession of collectors was a Welsh priest called Nennius, who put together, in about the year 800, all the traditional matter available to him. In doing so he preserved for us both myth and history, and indeed seemed quite unable, himself, to distinguish between the two. Because he did not actually compose the bulk of his collection himself, but copied it from unknown and various sources, we cannot precisely date all his material; we should particularly like to because his may be the first mention of Arthur.

There is no doubt, from the point of view of mythology, that the greatest and most important of the periodic reappraisals of the material was that made by Geoffrey of Monmouth, who wrote his 'History of the Kings of Britain' in or near 1136. He drew from known works such as those of Gildas, Nennius and Bede, from many other sources both written and remembered, and also very greatly from his own imagination, or that of some unidentified immediate predecessor.

Myths are by nature universal, because the same things happen to different people in different places and at different times, within a very restricted framework, that of human life. Yet where they occur they embody and express in a strong and pure form the particular character and temperament of the people they belong to, and the nature of the land they live in. Read the Icelandic sagas and you cannot help smelling the sheep-grazed grass at the edges of the melting snow and the resinous wooden homesteads on the shores of cold bays. The Eddas call up stony plateaux above wolf-packed pine forests; and elsewhere the god Lugh rides with the Riders of the Sidhe through a land pungent with the incense of turf fires. The early British myths which are located in North Wales are no exception, so that although it is clear that we are dealing with a branch of a distinct European tradition, and at the same time tapping the pool of world mythology, yet there is a certain feeling about the way the matter is formed, just as there is a certain feeling about the view of Snowdon from Llynnau Mymbyr, or the smell of heather on the Migneint, which makes you know, if you have any sensitivity at all, exactly where you are.

Old Gods in Gwynedd

It seems likely from place names and from surviving pockets of language that the people of ancient western Europe at one time spoke a single tongue. We call this Celtic, and the people who spoke it the Celts, although these are inevitably not very accurate or precise terms. We are encouraged to think of these people as a cohesive group by the similarity of their artefacts, which may indicate a similarity of way of life, outlook and social forms.

In Britain itself there came to be two main groups of the Celtic languages spoken, Goidelic or Gaelic in what is now Scotland, a language introduced there in the post-Roman period by invading tribes from Ireland, and Brythonic, the language of the Britons, the ancestor of the present Welsh tongue, which was spoken throughout the country up to Strathclyde and the Roman wall and remained widely spoken in the north of Britain for some centuries after the formation of the first English kingdoms. The original inhabitants of Scotland, known to the Romans and subsequent writers as the Picts, remain something of a mystery. Bede, writing in the 8th century, constantly distinguishes the Britons from the English, and refers to the peoples and provinces of Britain as "speaking the four languages, British, Pictish, Scottish and English."

The term 'British' today can not be used in quite the same sense, having come to absorb the whole lot of us, the original natives and the subsequent colonists, including the Normans. Consequently 'British' now fails to make the distinction, which all the early writers used it to make, between the natives of the island and the later comers. We have to use phrases such as 'native British' now to achieve that. To some (though a much lesser) extent, the term 'Britons' suffers the same handicap, since we are all Britons now, regardless of our provenance. That, however, was the term ('Britones') consistently used by all the first sources, writing as they were, of course, in Latin. Perhaps the most accurate thing one can say on the subject is that the people who were regarded by the

Romans and the early English as the original inhabitants of 'insula Britannia' were identified by their speaking the Brythonic branch of the Celtic languages, which thus has a special claim to be the medium of our original national culture.

Unfortunately we hear nothing about these people and their ways until it is almost too late for the news to be useful, because, in this relatively impoverished side of Europe, there was nobody suitable there to tell us. We have no early-Celtic Homer. In fact we have only Julius Caesar, viewing his enemy with suprising objectivity, even while systematically destroying the way of life he recorded. That was in the last decades before this era, and by then the traditions which he noted had been evolving in western Europe for at least two thousand years.

One thing which impressed Caesar was the strength of the oral culture. Writing had reached the western Celts by his day, but the habit of memorizing and reciting had, it seems, become such a characteristic of the tradition that it could not be discarded. The Druids, he said, believed that their religion prohibited them from committing their teachings to writing, and he attributed this to the esoteric nature of the material. Caesar gives us some clues as to what the Druids actually taught. Like the Aryan tribes who became eventually the Hindus they believed that the soul is immortal and subject to endless reincarnation in body after body. They were also, it seems, astronomers, perhaps even astrologers; and they dealt with the functions and characteristics of the gods.

Caesar names these gods, but in translation. The Celts, he said, worshipped Apollo, Mars, Jupiter and Minerva, in much the same way as the Romans. Clearly they did not, but we can only identify the gods to which he gives these confident Roman names by analogy of their functions. We do know from this record, however, that the Celtic peoples worshipped personified deities.

'In Britannia reperta atque inde in Galliam translata existimatur,' he says of the religion of the Druids: 'it was thought to have originated in Britain and to have been taken to Gaul from there.' People still, he tells us, go to Britain if they wish to study it in depth.

It would be surprising indeed if all trace of this body of thought had disappeared. There are some clues that it has not, and that instead of dying it became disguised, lay dormant in a sub-culture to reappear in thoroughly Christian times in the form of stories.

There was inevitably much that was new about the Welsh bardic tradition which emerged from the 'Dark Ages' following the Roman withdrawal and began to flower again in the early medieval period. It did not, however, come from nowhere. It was itself part of the continuity of the oral tradition, the long and indestructible chain of memory which Caesar noted. It may be seen, then, as in part at least representing the rebirth in a new form of the lore of the Druids.

In one story in particular we can discern something more archaic than the heroic events which others appear to retell. It is there, if anywhere, that the remnants of the gods of the Celts are to be found.

In the great treasury of stories known as the Mabinogion, 'Math, son of Mathonwy' stands out as both the most complex and the most intriguing. It is moreover so explicitly located in the weather-swept country of the extreme west of North Wales that it seems to present the memory of a cult which once flourished there.

The story concerns a king of Gwynedd, Math, and Gwydion, his sister's son, known to the tale as Gwydion son of Don. Both these figures are portrayed as magicians of great power, and in the opening episode Gwydion plays a complicated trick on his uncle by acquiring the sacred swine of Pryderi, king of South Wales. He then makes an epic journey to the north with the sacred animals, and finds on arrival that he has succeeded in his ploy, which was to cause war between North and South Wales. His journey with the swine is said to be commemorated by the names of places where he stopped, for example Mochdre, 'pig town', near Colwyn Bay.

This war ends with a hand-to-hand fight between the two leaders, Gwydion and Pryderi, face to face in front of their armies, an event which is set on that great stretch of estuarial marsh, now reclaimed and tamed, which forms the silt-plain of the river

Glaslyn as it drains the Snowdon range into Tremadog Bay — Y Traeth Mawr, then a stretch of tidal beach.

Several other specific spots in this small area are named in this episode: the southern army had retreated to Nant Call, which is near Beddgelert; they dropped back further to Dôl Benmaen, west of where Tremadog now is. A spot on the river Dwyryd in the Vale of Ffestiniog, known as Rhyd y Pedestri, appears to refer to an event mentioned in the story: 'the men on foot' in the rival armies began shooting at each other there.

The ancient woodland of the Ffestiniog valley is well suited to be the home of such references. But it is up at the church of Maentwrog above it that we come face to face with a link between pre-history and the surviving stories. Pryderi, 'Math' tells, was killed by Gwydion on Traeth Mawr, 'and at Maen Tyriawg, above Y Felenrhyd, was he buried, and his grave is there.'

Set into the wall of the church at Maentwrog is something known as 'Twrog's stone'. It is a rounded monolith, similar in form to

Traeth Mawr, once a beach of the Glaslyn estuary, now reclaimed land, where the leaders Gwydion and Pryderi faced each other in front of their armies.

'Twrog's stone' is an apparently prehistoric pillar embedded in the wall of Maentwrog church, perhaps the burial place of Pryderi.

those sometimes found in burial chambers. Clearly prehistoric, its presence there indicates that the church was built on the site of a previously sacred monument, perhaps a burial chamber of which only this pillar remains; and if so, perhaps the one referred to in the story as the burial place of Pryderi.

A new figure then enters the tale, whose exploits are to be even more firmly tied to the land of Gwynedd. Arianrhod, sister of the magician Gwydion, is a powerful and sinister personage, who has not a little of the goddess of death about her. When we first meet her she fails in a test of her virginity: when asked to step over Math's magic staff she drops two children. The first is a fine boy child who leaves the story at once by running into the sea, where he becomes aquatic and gains the name Dylan Eil Don, 'Sea son of Wave'. The spot where this extraordinary event took place can be identified on the coast south of Caernarfon, where a headland is still called Maen Dylan, 'Dylan's stone', (where an exceptionally large boulder lies on the beach, together with another which one might fancy to be fish-like in shape, just off the end of the headland), at Pontllyfni, just south of Pen-y-groes.

The second child is described as a small object, which Gwydion takes up (as Arianrhod flees in shame) and hides in a chest. It is a boy, who grows at a remarkable rate, and Gwydion has him reared. The story then moves into its central phase when he takes the prodigious child to confront his mother at her castle, Caer Arianrhod.

There are two ways one can see Caer Arianrhod today. One is to look up in the sky, where it is the name of the Corona Borealis, the 'northern crown', a small uncomplete circle of stars in the northern sky between the constellations of Boötes and Hercules. Interestingly this same group of stars is said in Greek mythology to be the silver circlet of Ariadne, indicating that these two goddesses with similar names may originally have been one and the same.

The other way to see Caer Arianrhod is to stand on top of the ring fort of Dinas Dinlle (itself, as we shall see, called after her son) and look out to sea. There at very low tide a reef of stone appears, all that remains, it is said, of her sunken city.

Maen Dylan is a strange boulder lying off the end of a promontory near Pontllyfni, a spot associated with the boy Dylan who took on the sea's nature and leapt into the waves.

The corona borealis is a constellation in the northern sky which has the name Caer Arianrhod in Welsh and is said in Greek mythology to be the circlet of Ariadne. Caer Arianrhod is also a formation of large rocks visible at low tide off the coast near Llandwrog.

This physical remnant of the mythical city lies a short distance off-shore just south-west of Morfa Dinlle, on the coast between Llandwrog and Clynnog. It has been investigated in some detail, and the probability seems to be that it is a denuded 'drumlin', a lump of land left by a glacier and eroded by the sea. Ashton, however, who recorded his investigations of 1909 in his book 'The Evolution of a Coastline', was convinced that it was an ancient British stone circle, a supposition which would match the monolith at Maen Twrog and help to explain how this feature off the south-Caernarfon coast comes to be in this ancient story.

This son of Arianrhod's whom Gwydion brought to confront her, walking 'along the seashore between there and Aber Menai', became the hero of the rest of the tale, Lleu Llaw Gyffes, who gave his name to that immense ring-fort, now partly fallen into the sea, Din-Lleu, now known as Dinas Dinlle, the place where he was supposedly reared.

In fact the area as a whole displays the astonishing persistence of place-names, unless indeed these post-date the story rather than having been known by its teller. Just inland from Dinas Dinlle a farmstead under the lee of a most unusual hill crested by an outcrop of scrub bears the name Bryn Gwydion, so that we may fancy that this was the place where the wizard lived. As a striking illustration of the way names endure, a new housing estate in Llandwrog has been named Maes Gwydion. The dedication of that village church to Twrog is also of interest, as it gives us another link with the locations of the story, 'Twrog's stone' up at Maentwrog being perhaps identifiable, as we have just seen, as the burial place of Pryderi.

Dinas Dinlle, crumbling into the waves, overlooks a notably dull and dreary coastline, featureless except for this big hump and except for the distant views to Anglesey and the mountains of the Lleyn peninsula. It was, however, along this shore that Gwydion came with Lleu.

His mother imposed on Lleu a number of curses, one of which was that he should never have a wife of the human race. As a result of this the two wizards, Math and Gwydion, then perform a

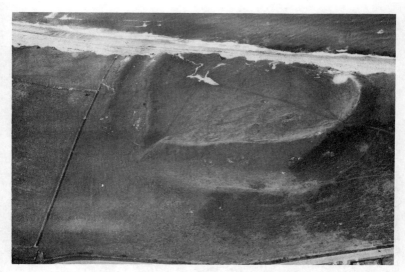

The ring fort of Dinas Dinlle, seat of the hero Lleu Llaw Gyffes, is now crumbling away under the sea's erosion, on the coast close to Llandwrog.

ceremony which must rank as one of the most appealing images in this generally imaginative mythology. They make for him a wife out of wild flowers, using those common and indigenous flora of the Welsh countryside in its flush of early summer — the flowers of the oak, the meadowsweet, and the broom. Out of this interesting combination they made the most beautiful woman ever seen. They called her Blodeuwedd, from the Welsh 'blodau', flowers.

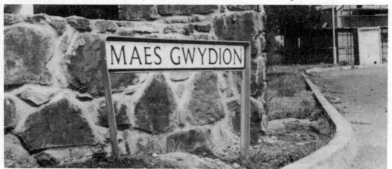

The name of the wizard Gwydion is still remembered today in the area of his home.

Bryn Gwydion.

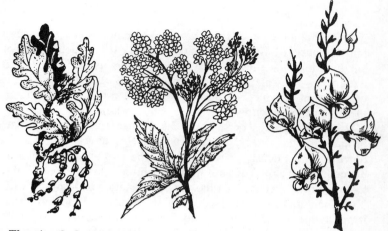

The wizards Gwydion and Math made for Lleu a wife out of the common Welsh flowers, the flowers of the oak, the meadowsweet and the broom.

Lleu's name is kept alive in Nantlle(u) — "Lleu's Valley"

Arianrhod now fades from the tale, and Blodeuwedd becomes a central figure. Math, the king of Gwynedd, gave to Lleu an area of his kingdom — the territory now known as Eifionydd and Ardudwy — to celebrate his marriage. 'The place in the cantref where he set up court was the place called Mur Castell, and that in the uplands of Ardudwy.'

It is symptomatic, perhaps, of the strangeness of the contrasts brought about by the passage of time, that this same spot now looks down onto a nuclear power station. The site is now known as Tomen y Mur, and consists of a large mound on an exposed hill, looking down over the lake and the power station of Trawsfynydd. Not much can be said of it with certainty, but there is no doubt that it was at one time a Roman camp. The ruins of Roman baths exist nearby, and the outline of something thought to have been a small amphitheatre. The mound itself which forms its most compelling feature is said to be the motte of a medieval castle, a common enough feature throughout North Wales and the border country. The fact that it looks so much like a large burial mound, being particularly reminiscent of the Irish mounds on the river Boyne, tempts us to speculate, though without any firm evidence, that it may have been an older structure re-used as a convenient basis for a motte.

Apart from that one striking piece of change, not much can have altered in the country around Tomen y Mur in the centuries since the Romans shivered there, or indeed in the millennia which have passed since the time when Lleu and Blodeuwedd were (as seems probable) the deities of living people. The place is isolated by its wildness. Across the lake the grey hills block one horizon, and to the east a long expanse of marsh and reed rises towards open moorland. The story too has an indestructible, defiant permanence about it.

Up at that court alone, while her husband Lleu was away, Blodeuwedd took as a lover a neighbouring lord (Gronw Pebyr, lord of Penllyn at the end of Bala lake) who happened to be passing, much as Helen of Troy invited Paris in, at the court of Sparta, while her husband Menelaus was away on business. The lover in

Tomen y Mur, the 'Mur Castell' where Lleu lived with Blodeuwedd, combines a Roman fort with a medieval motte.

Detail of stone wall at Tomen y Mur today.

such cases finds himself in the ambiguous position of being a guest in the absent rival's house. In spite of this assumed obligation they plot to dispose of Lleu on his return. This matter, however, is made more complicated by another familiar theme. Lleu is a hero of the type who can only be killed under certain circumstances — a reference, perhaps, to ritual of some sort, perhaps originally human sacrifice.

This theme, it seems, combines the element of narrative interest — we know that he will die, we know that it is apparently impossible, and we wait to see how it can be done — with the deeply intriguing idea of a predestined fate being unavoidable, just as Achilles was doomed to die in the Trojan War and could not evade it even by his almost total invulnerability: his only mortal portion, his heel, would inevitably produce his destined death. In Lleu's case this issue contains two further mythic themes, the winkling out of him by Blodeuwedd, Delilah-like, of his fateful secret; and the theme of being between two worlds, where things are neither this nor that, a theme which recurs in superstition and ritual, such as the belief that ghosts walk at midnight (neither one day nor the other) and witches fly at Halloween, the junction of the summer and the winter parts of the pagan year, a time also of licence and the breaking of taboos.

Lleu Llaw Gyffes can be killed neither within a house nor outside, neither on horseback nor on foot, and (it appears) neither on water nor on dry land. Blodeuwedd lures him into telling her how these contraries can be reconciled, and as a result we find him in due course trustingly perched, with one foot on the back of a he-goat and the other on the edge of a bath-tub, under a canopy of thatch on the bank of the river Cynfal near their home.

The Cynfal is a fast-flowing, busy stream, in an often deep valley, which runs down from the moors above Ffestiniog and Trawsfynydd, to pass under the road which runs between those two places. The story says specifically that the lover and conspirator hid himself 'under the lee of a hill which is now called Bryn Cyfergyr', and indeed there is a hill called (now) 'Bryn Cyfergyd' there still, a remarkable and striking feature, a

The treacherous lover Gronw hid in ambush behind the hill called Bryn Cyfergyr (now Bryn Cyfergyd), still a notable knoll overlooking the Cynfal valley.

Below Bryn Cyfergyd the Cynfal river falls into a wooded gorge.

prominent knoll at a vantage point overlooking the steep deep valley. It seems in fact that there are several places in this immediate area which may bear references to the story. An old farmhouse among meadows near the valley bottom is called Bron Goronwy, possibly after the lover Gronw, and perched on a hill high above the river another property known as Bryn Saeth may perhaps be a reference to the making of the special spear by which Gronw eventually killed Lleu. Against this attractive possibility it might be argued that 'saeth' means 'arrow', whereas the story specifies a spear ('gwaew.' in the Old Welsh text, modern Welsh 'gwayw'). A little further down, another stream arrives to form an area which is almost an island and is known as Ynys Las, and it is there that the hero has been considered by some people to have set up his bath-tub and goat.

The Cynfal is a remarkable river, even among the many striking and evocative mountain streams which so vividly seam North Wales. It drops from its source in the Migneint with spectacular viguour, releasing in a succession of waterfalls one which deserves to be famous, and performs several quick changes of nature before it surges into our story. By that time it lies deep in its own carved valley, some slopes of which have now unfortunately been planted with alien softwood. Between Bryn Cyfergyd and Ynys Las it undergoes a sudden transformation, leaping from an open, hilly moorland mode to an idyllic bosky one, running out of craggy country straight into a world of natural woodland, scrub oak carpetted by bilberry bushes, lavish with pools and waterfalls.

This is a place of considerable drama and sensation. The movement and fall of the river give a combined visual and audible effect which sets up an atmosphere filling the deep wood. In the summer the sunlight cascades through leaves and splashes back up from the surfaces of pools to ripple on the rock walls above them. Sometimes in the winter some of the smaller falls freeze and become hanging trailers, while the ivy pouring from the rocks turns white with frost and mimics waterfalls. It is in fact a place of intriguing ambiguity, of depths of shade and cateracts of light, of boiling turbulence and calm pools, but one thing that is not at all ambiguous about it is its total antiquity. Commercial afforestation invades its borders, and the occasional detritus of household refuse mars its rock-pools, but the climate of primal woodland dominates this stretch of the Cynfal valley still.

These explicit toponymic associations, such as the knoll Bryn Cyfergyd and perhaps some others in this valley, a valley itself clearly the one in the story, seem to demand some explanation. On the one hand the known durability of place-names — perhaps amongst the oldest of the artefacts of our countryside — raises the possibility that they have actually been known by those names all that time, whatever that is, the time perhaps which has elapsed since a local cult gained a more than local influence and the early deities of this area became encapsulated in popular tales. There are of course a few alternatives, particularly as we do not know for certain how old the place-names actually are. The title deeds of the respective farms, which were all at one time part of the Pengwern estate, were lost in a distant fire. The farm properties may indeed have been named by someone with a knowledge of the Mabinogion, though it must be said that the local people now do not on the whole recognise the connection. Oddly, the Mabinogion means little or nothing to them. Alternatively the story-teller to whom we owe the surviving record of apparently ancient matter may for personal reasons have decided to locate the occurrences here, and much of the rest of 'Math' around this same part of Gwynedd, and picked for the purpose spots in this most naturally numinous place.

It is not to be supposed, I think, that the related events ever actually took place, unless as some sort of religious ritual, so that we need nor worry about the impossibility of that long spear-shot from the lee of Bryn Cyfergyd through a terrain quite probably more treed once than even now, down to the tumbling river way below, or, (in the alternative scenario which we shall be considering shortly in the light of recent events), across a half-mile of hillside. The ritualistic or symbolic air of the whole thing is clear enough, and if for narrative reasons it must be thought of as having actually happened, and therefore as having happened somewhere, there can be no more suitable place for us to imagine it than here.

Lleu, struck through with a spear in this highly ritualistic scene on the Cynfal, flies to heaven in the form of an eagle — a reference, perhaps, to a belief in the transmigration of souls. His betrayal, however, does not go unpunished. His uncle and patron Gwydion searches the forests for the eagle-Lleu, and having found him perched in a tree in the Nantlle valley below Snowdon uses his magic arts to restore him to human form. The two then vengefully approach the heights of Tomen y Mur, where Blodeuwedd waits with her maidens.

Knowing they are coming, she and the maidens set off from the court in fear, cross the mountain and the Cynfal river in its upper cwm, and flee towards the moorland. Foolishly they all looked back in fear as they went, with the result that the maidens, walking ahead, stumbled backwards into a lake and were drowned. Llyn Morwynion, 'lake of the maidens', still lies up there, a shallow moorland lake with a lip overlooking not only the upper Cynfal but a fine distant view down to Traeth Mawr and the Porthmadog coast, and out beyond the bay to the Lleyn peninsula. To come up over that edge and onto the moorland backwards would be quite demanding, but then to proceed to fall into the lake would require an unusual degree of carelessness. Their mistress, in any case, did not follow her maidens to that end. And there it was, at the edge of that moorland lake, that Gwydion caught Blodeuwedd up.

She was confronted not only by his terrible and rightful anger, but by his magic powers. He turned her there and then into an owl — yet another reference, in this story so rich in allusion, to the belief in the transmigration of souls. An owl she still is, and you can hear her in the Welsh woods bemoaning her fate. 'Blodeuwedd' is, the tale says, still 'owl' in our language, and it may once have been, meaning as it does 'flower-face'.

The lover, meanwhile, all too aware of his likely fate, retreated towards Bala, and sent messages to Lleu offering compensation. These were haughtily refused, and instead Lleu demanded that he undergo the same trial as he did, standing as target on the banks of

The upper Cynfal valley.

Llyn Morwynion is a moorland lake with a lip high over the Cynfal valley, the spot where Blodeuwedd's maidens drowned.

the Cynfal. As it seems every man has done since Adam, he sought forgiveness by blaming the woman for having set him up. To some extent Lleu relented, and allowed him the chance of holding a stone between him and the spear-blow. To no avail; the spear went straight through it, and through him: 'And there the stone is, on the bank of Cynfal river in Ardudwy, and the hole through it.'

That statement is clear enough, and we cannot help believing that when it was written (in the version we have, in the late 14th century) there was such a stone there. Over the course of time, though, the stone's whereabouts seem to have become forgotten. Perhaps it was obscured by moss or covered over by leaf-mould. Perhaps it was simply no longer there — broken up to make a wall, or removed by some ancient souvenir hunter? Not through lack of searching, many of us had come to this conclusion; indeed I said as much in a previous publication, 'Portrait of North Wales'.

We were encouraged in this belief by the total lack of any evidence of the stone having been seen in modern times. Lady Charlotte Guest, in her otherwise comprehensive notes to her edition of the Mabinogion in 1848, makes no mention of the stone. A writer called Frank Ward wrote in 1935 that it had been said in 1830 that a stone answering the description had stood on the banks of the Cynfal within living memory. After extensive searching he himself found a slab with a hole in it, at the time filled with moss, but since it measured only forty to forty-two inches in height it does not form an adequate representative of Gronw's Stone, and in any case it has not been found again since. Modern searchers have been consistently unsuccessful — that is, until the early weeks of 1990.

A local teacher and historian, Geraint Vaughan Jones, who had been looking around the area for the stone for some time, was up on the hillside with a friend attempting to trace the route of Sarn Helen in its passage across the Cynfal valley, when quite by accident they found what appears to be the stone referred to. When found it was half buried and the hole was covered with moss but still visible. The most likely explanation for it not having been found before is that it is apparently in the wrong place. It lies not beside the Cynfal but alongside a small tributary, one of several

Llech Ronw — 'Gronw's Stone'.

such tributaries of the Cynfal which drain the southern slopes of its valley. The stream in question runs not far from the farm Bryn Saeth, the name of which is supposed to refer to the making of the spear.

It is a smooth, nearly rectangular but slightly tapered slab, some five foot six inches in length from toe to head, with a hole about four and a half inches in diameter approximately five inches from the head. It has since been shown that if a six-foot man stands behind it, the hole is very much in the area of his heart.

Bryn Saeth is in view of the site of the stone, and along the forest edge can be seen Bryn Cyfergyd itself, though its distance of at least half a mile implies an accurate as well as a forceful spear-shot. The tale says that the place is known as Llech Ronw, Gronw's Stone, and indeed the farm immediately above the spot is still called Llech Goronwy. Mr Vaughan Jones, who found the stone, was told a curious story by a lady now in her seventies whose grandfather farmed the land at Llech Goronwy. When his sons were cutting hay, which they did then with scythes, he always forbade them to mow a mound near the farmhouse, because he said that was the burial mound of Gronw Bebyr. Unfortunately although she showed him the site of the mound the area has been so disturbed by forestry that it cannot now be seen.

As a site for the strange events, this elevated open slope is much more credible than the deep tree-choked gorge of the main river. It is perhaps the last point along this bank which can be seen from Bryn Cyfergyd. The story does not say that the goat-and-bathtub death and its repeat performance took place actually on the river, though one naturally assumes this; it simply says that it was on 'the far side of the river, facing Bryn Cyfergyr', which this site is. There remains the problem of the categorical statement by the story-teller: 'And there the stone is, on the bank of the Cynfal river in Ardudwy . . .' He could of course simply have got his geography wrong, but this would be inconsistent with his other accuracies and his evident knowledge of the neighbourhood.

There are various possible ways out of this dilemma. One such is to take the name 'the Cynfal river' to include its close tributaries, which may indeed not have borne individual names, although the stream by which the stone was actually found is now known after the farm nearby as Afon Bryn Saeth. Another would be to translate the Welsh phrase 'ar lan Afon Cynfal' not 'on the bank of' but 'on the valley slope of', which is perhaps not too far-fetched and would perfectly describe the location.

It would be interesting to know (though we never shall) what was the order of cause and effect, between the stone and the tale. The hole in the stone appears to be old and man-made. It is not the sort of smooth yet irregular hole which could be worn by water. It is even and round and neither rough nor smooth, but consistently worked, as if with a small chisel. Yet though an apparent artefact it does not seem capable of any clear purpose, being too large to take a hinge for a gate; and in any case the slab is not long enough to make a gate-post, a large part of which must be sunk below ground to give it stability.

There are two possible directions for the chain of events which located the strange episodes at this spot. There might have been the given phenomenon of a stone with an unexplained hole, for which a detail added to a tale could give an explanation. Alternatively the tale in which Lleu's spear pierces Gronw's stone might have become so prestigious that the motive arose for supporting it with the evidence of a stone, although one would then have to ask why it was put just here.

We know, then, where these remote figures of myth, Gwydion, Arianrhod, Lleu, were said to have been when the events connected with them occurred, almost to a few yards being able to locate the bizarre episodes on the banks of the Cynfal or the confrontation of Gwydion and Blodeuwedd. Perhaps partly for this reason we feel tantalised by not knowing more about them, where they came from, who they originally were. Confused as it is the story does, however, give us some clues, and the background tradition fills in some of the gaps.

We have seen that Caer Arianrhod is something more than a reef of stones off the Gwynedd coast. Through its name and its connection with the Corona Borealis it connects Arianrhod with Ariadne. There is another reference to Caer Arianrhod in the riddle of Taliesin (whom we shall meet again), from which it may be argued that the circlet of stars is regarded as the otherworld to which souls go after death, and where they reside before birth, which would make Arianrhod a sort of goddess of death.

A more powerful clue as to the characters' identity lies in the name given in the story for the parent of both Gwydion and Arianrhod, who are referred to as the children of Don, interestingly not a male personage originally but a goddess, and so intended to be seen as Math's sister. Apart from this interesting indication of matrilinear descent, the mention of the goddess Don brings the story directly to the heart of European myth.

Don is identified as the same deity as the Irish goddess Danann, of Danu, the mother of the gods, and the stories of her children therefore probably formed, in Britain, an equivalent branch of myth to the Irish tales of the people of the goddess Danann, mythical invaders of Ireland who no doubt correspond, in the looser time-scale of myth, to one of several major waves of colonisation which we know to have taken place during the Bronze Age and Iron Age. We have reason to suppose that whoever these people were, the children of Don or Danann were widespread and powerful in Europe at the end of the Bronze Age.

We know that Don or Danann was no merely local deity. We know this because of the distribution of the name in European place-names. To begin with, the goddess has given her name to several rivers, not just the two or three examples in England and France but one of Europe's major rivers, which flows to the east of the Ukraine down to Rostov, emerging into the Sea of Azov, (a corner of the Black Sea), still called the river Don.

Two other Black Sea rivers, the Dnieper and the Dniester, are also thought to have been called after her. But most significant of all is her claim to the Danube, in the basin of which came into being those cultures, known to archeologists as the 'Urnfield' and later the 'Hallstatt' cultures, which form the roots of the recognisable style associated with the Celtic-speaking peoples. Traditionally these people spread out from the Danube, and indeed our earliest reference to them, by Herodotus in the fifth century B.C., mentions them in direct connection with the source of that river.

If all this is correct then Don is a person of some importance. We would therefore expect the other characters who fall under her auspices in the tale to be of significance too; and we would not be disappointed. Lleu himself, the hero of the story of Math, is thought to be the Welsh version of the Irish god Lugh, who, skilled, clever and inventive, may be seen as the Celtic equivalent of Mercury or Hermes. As the general European god Lugus he gave his name to places as far apart as Lyon, Leiden and Carlisle.

With Gwydion we are on less sure ground. Both his main features and his name connect him with the Scandinavian god noted for trickery and magic, and connected with wisdom and warfare, Odin, or in his Teutonic form Woden. And these too shared their characteristics of trickery with Mercury, whom Tacitus cites as the main deity of the Gauls. It is agreed, in fact, from an early date, that Mercury and Woden were equivalent, to the extent that the Germans translated the Roman 'Mercurii dies' as Woden's-day.

Both Gwydion and Lleu may then be variants of the same principle, represented elsewhere by Lugh and Woden, the god of cunning, recorded by the Romans as being the main god of the European Celts, and what we see taking place in Gwynedd in the tale of Math may be the superimposition of the worship of a later variant on a still surviving older cult, rather as Judaism and Christianity at certain times and places co-existed.

The Romans Leave

A few of the great events and periods in the early life of a country stick in its memory for ever. Thus we have never forgotten that for some four hundred years of our childhood as a nation we were subject to the pedagogic authority of Rome. Perhaps what was so incisive about the Roman occupation was that it was clearly bounded. They came and they went. The seeing and the conquering occurred between fixed limits. They never became Britons, nor, completely, did the Britons become Romans. Yet it could hardly be the case that the people of Britain do not include in their attitudes and outlooks the influence of those four centuries of occupation.

Rome is consequently in the background of much of the mythology, and not least the mythology of North Wales. One of our stories exemplifies to perfection the perceived relation between ancient Britain and Rome. At the same time it provides a clear and fascinating example of the way myth transforms history to make it accessible in simple story form and comprehensible to an audience more accustomed to stories than to facts.

The Romans did not expand to Ireland, and they walled off Scotland, but Wales was, for tactical and political reasons, thoroughly invaded. The subsequent history of each of these three places has no doubt been affected by these variations in their treatment. The early tradition of Wales, in any case, shows a consciousness of the need to recognise Rome's influential presence.

Perhaps it is because the Romans penetrated even into the mountainous heartland of North Wales that myth finds it necessary to deal with them there, as if taking the extremest case. The story which encapsulates the whole period, from arrival to departure, in a single simple image, is 'The Dream of Lord Macsen'. A finely crafted, delicately balanced work, it is full of British imagery and style. Yet it starts off, with great courage and imagination, in the countryside around Rome.

The Emperor Macsen has gone out hunting with his retinue of subject kings, and because of the great heat in the middle of the day he had a canopy raised over him, and fell asleep. As he slept, in that Italian river valley, he had a dream. He dreamt that he was travelling across another country, then on a sea voyage which took him to an island, 'the loveliest in the world', when he then crossed to its further shore. Here he came to a rough and mountainous land full of steep slopes and crags. From the heights of that land he could see another island near the shore, and at the mouth of a river flowing towards the sea he saw a great castle. He went down and entered it, and found it to be richly furnished. The daughter of the house came forward to greet him, and in his dream he sat down with her in a golden chair. At that moment of the dream, with his arms around her and their cheeks together, the story says, 'What with the dogs straining at their leashes, and the edges of the shields banging against each other, and the spear shafts hitting together, and the stamping and neighing of the horses, the Emperor woke'. The poor man found that he was so in love with the girl he had dreamt of that no part of him, down to the tips of his fingernails, was free of that love. In great depression he rode back to Rome, and during the next week his lack of appetite and spirit began to worry his attendants.

Eventually Macsen reveals his dream and sends out messengers to find the place of it, and after an initial year of failure they at last find the route he dreamt he took. They cross the sea in the ship he used in his dream, and come to the island of Britain. Travelling across the island, they reach the mountains of the west, and having penetrated these they see ahead of them the island of Anglesey, and the land of Arfon in between. They see the river Seiont, with a castle at its mouth, and find within that everything exactly as the Emperor had described. Falling on their knees before the woman they had come to find, they proclaim her Empress of Rome.

Given the choice of going to Rome or awaiting the Emperor in Arfon, the lady very reasonably expressed slight scepticism about the whole thing, and suggested that if the Emperor really loved her he had better come to Wales.

It was as a result of this that the Romans came to Britain. The Emperor arriving, the tale says, conquered the king of Britain, Beli, and drove him and his people into the sea. Without pausing he then went on to Arfon. He recognised the land as soon as he saw it, and the castle at the mouth of the river Seiont, and he went straight in to marry his Empress. As a wedding present she asked, among other things, for three strongholds to be made for her, one here in Arfon, the other two at Caerfyrddin and Caer Lleon. In these latter we recognise, of course, the two chief Roman forts of Wales, Carmarthen and Caerleon.

The one with which the story deals in particular, the fortress in Arfon, now lies a little way from the river Seiont, which has moved, but nevertheless still bears its name, in the Romanised form of Segontium. Navigable once, the river's mouth has silted. Looking down from it today onto the water of the Menai Strait, on the town of Caernarfon beside the shore, and indeed (since the Roman site is slightly raised in relation to the shore-level) over the tops of the towers of King Edward's impressive and famous castle, you still get a strong feeling of its water-based location.

That Segontium should have been chosen as a representative Roman site by the mythology perhaps reflects its distinction in being so far west, deep in the heartland where the myths accumulated. In fact, despite the naming of it in Nennius' history as one of the twenty-eight cities of the island, it was never really a town, let alone a city. Rather it was an auxiliary fort, one of the many outposts of the regional fortress at Chester, although in its final phase it seems large enough to have been a centre of local administration in its own right. It was also surrounded by a haphazard accretion of the dwellings of traders and their families, rather as a shanty town inevitably grows up around the intentionally planned town in so many parts of the modern world.

Just as the fort presents us with the physical basis of the origins of the myth in the realm of geography, so the recorded facts provide us with a view of its origins in history. Events recorded by Tacitus as having taken place in the summer of 78 AD bring this part of North Wales into the mainstream of Roman history.

The Roman fort of Segontium occupies a large area near the river Seiont outside Caernarfon.

The face of Magnus Maximus, the Macsen of Welsh myth, may still be seen on a coin in the Segontium museum.

The Silures had been subdued in the rather easier fighting country of South Wales. Their equivalent tribe in the north, however, the Ordovices, which occupied the inland parts of North Wales, had succeeded in decimating a troop of Roman cavalry, an achievement which must have meant much to morale on both sides. As autumn approached it seemed that this state of play would be the governing one for the rest of that year. Events were to be decided in the end, however, not by climate or terrain but by the character of the new governor, Agricola, who seems to have been decisive, daring, and determined. He decided on a spearhead thrust into the heart of the land which was harbouring the resistance. The Ordovices wisely took to the hills, but Agricola was not put off by their natural advantage there. Tacitus tells us that he himself led his men into the hills; but Tacitus was his son-in-law. He also says that the assault succeeded in destroying almost the whole fighting force of the Ordovices. How much of this is Roman self-congratulation we do now know for certain. We do know that the building of Roman forts along the strategic routes through North Wales was the immediate result, and that Segontium was among them.

It was not, then, through love that the Emperor came, nor out of a blissful marriage in an adopted country that he remained. The original wooden field-fort at Segontium was greatly strengthened during the next hundred years, indicating increased rather than decreased danger and need for control. The new stone-built fort, with its excellent access by sea, turned out to be a crucial link in the network which remained as at least a constant threat to overt insurrection throughout Wales until the fourth century AD. The story of Macsen summarises the arrival and the staying of the Romans, but it is to their final leaving that it relates most closely.

The Emperor, it tells us, stayed in Britain for seven years, as a result of which a new Emperor was proclaimed in Rome. When Macsen heard of this he gathered an army and set out to restore his rule, conquering France, Burgundy and Italy before laying siege to Rome itself. It was eventually the troops from Britain who came with him ('Better fighters were in that small host than twice their

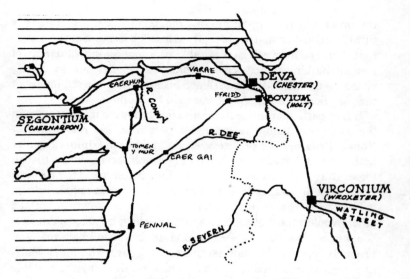

number of Romans') that won the city. They did this by making
use of a cultural difference between the two forces. The Romans
would take their main meal at midday, but the Britons favoured a
large breakfast. It was thus at one noontime, while both Emperors
were eating, that they went over the ramparts. So it was the Britons
who took Rome, and only as a gesture of generosity did they give it
back to the rightful Emperor and his British wife.

Part of the charm of the story is its innocent simplicity, which
can represent the invasion, occupation, and evacuation of Britain
by Rome all in terms of a tale of love. What the tale summarises in
this way was in fact a long and complicated process, the several
phases and waves of Roman invasion and also the various native
British actions in continental Europe. In all this there are several
elements which can be clearly identified, both in history and in
myth. In the latter sphere, we have references to deeply-rooted
mythic material, such as the statement that Beli was king of Britain
when the Romans came. Beli was in fact a Celtic god, so that what is
no doubt being said is that the pre-Roman island was still subject to
the traditional religion. The story also shows an understanding of

41

the process of the imposition of Roman systems onto an already firmly established native order, the partial absorption of the one by the other; and it reveals an inevitable awareness of the solid relics of Roman buildings themselves, which, since they are so clearly visible to us still today, must have been remarkable reminders of the significance of the long visit paid by Rome.

It is of particular interest, in this connection, that the Macsen in the story undeniably represents a person in the real world of Roman Britain, to be precise a certain Magnus Maximus, a soldier under Count Theodosius who found himself serving in the British forces during the second half of the fourth century. He had been born in Spain, and his presence here in itself seems to proclaim him to be something of an adventurer, one of those willing to undertake other people's wars in places in which they have no natural interest. We know that he did well, rising to commanding rank and probably leading the successful assaults against the Picts which immediately preceded his entry into history. Bede says he was able and energetic. He certainly needed to be to achieve what he then did.

It seems that the island had become rather remote from central attention, and dissatisfaction with the rule of the Emperor Gratian exploded into a rebellion in which Maximus' troops proclaimed him Emperor, early in the year 383. Whatever his own part in this sudden elevation may have been, he was quick to make use of it. At once he invaded Gaul, taking with him not only his own legion but whatever auxiliary troops he could get. By the end of the summer he had killed the Emperor and established his own court. The largely British force then held Gaul for the next four years, after which, reinforced from Britain, it moved into Italy. In the meantime the Empire had come to recognise his *de facto* imperiality. By the early part of the next year, 388, the British rebels were in Rome.

For Britain the real significance of this was not that achievement, but the fact that the Romans had, in the process of invading Europe, left the island. As an effective occupying force they had gone. This, which might have seemed a long-awaited blessing, in fact filled the remaining islanders with dismay. A great deal had changed during the last period of occupation, as is quite clear from the massive strength of the forts of the 'Saxon Shore', built during the hundred years preceding Maximus' revolt. The wholesale removal of the island's fighting forces must have given the civilian inhabitants adequate cause for terror.

Such then was the reality, as opposed to the myth, of Britain's ironic turning of the tables against Rome. It was into such a situation that the Saxons then launched their increasingly strong invasions.

It is not without foundation that these events have been located by the tradition in Caernarfon. At Segontium we find considerable restoration shortly before the time of Maximus' rise to power, and then almost complete evacuation in the year of his invasion of Gaul, in 383. The dates are fairly accurately identifiable from the finds of coins, and the presence of a small garrison there up to the year 390 is attested in this way. Remarkably there was sufficient confidence in the reality of this new British-based Emperor and enough time and organisation for the native British rebels to mint their own coins, by which no doubt the soldiers left stranded at Segontium were paid. As a result we can see the face of the Emperor Magnus Maximus on a coin found there, a long-headed, high-browed, quite un-Roman face, with a small snubbed nose and a strong, thrusting chin. Not at all an unpleasant face or a proud or aggressive one, but rather that of a youngish, open-natured man.

Emperor-making was not a new occupation for the troops in Britain, since it had been achieved with great success in 306, when the legions garrisoned at York proclaimed as Emperor the man who was to become famous in history for his establishment of Christianity as the official religion of the Empire — Constantine the Great, the son of the Emperor Constantius, then serving in the army in Britain. There is a connection here with our tale, since it is that hero's mother, Helena, who returns as Macsen's bride, since her name is given in the Mabinogion story as Elen. This Roman-British figure is traditionally associated with the Roman roads, some of which bear her name to this day: Sarn Elen. With the suprising accuracy of ancient tradition this probably reflects the fact that it was under her husband, Constantius, and their son Constantine that the great network of roads became fully established — though as campaigning routes they had obviously been in existence since the time of Agricola, and even then frequently followed ancient trackways. After her marriage, says the tale, 'Elen thought to make high roads from one stronghold to another across the Island of Britain.'

Constantine's mother Helena was actually not from Britain, but probably of Asian origin. She seems to have become a well-known figure in her own right, to the extent of having coins minted in her name, and the discovery of twelve of these at Segontium testifies at least to a knowledge of her existence in these parts.

One further link connects Segontium with the story of Macsen. Just outside the Roman fort stands Caernarfon's parish church. A Mithraic temple nearby testifies to the area's early sacredness; its altar stone was found embedded in the church's south wall. This is the parish church of St Peblig, and the name continues the association between myth and fact. It comes from the Latin name Publicius, said to be none other than the son of Magnus Maximus himself.

Segontium itself is not now a very inspiring place, having the low-key, rather sterile air shared by most Roman ruins. It has a rather unattractive orderliness about it, no doubt originating from the meticulous grid-shape of its layout. More impressive are the remains of a subsidiary compound fortifying a landing place, built on the bank of the river to the west of the main fort, where walls still stand in people's gardens along South Road to almost their original Roman height.

Our local stretch of Sarn Elen, the landscape's other memorial of the people commemorated in the story, is perhaps more evocative. It forms a north-south link between the Roman forts, leaving Canovium on the Conwy to join the southern route from Segontium at a place we have already visited in this book, up at the moorland fort of Tomen y Mur. Across the hills and heather-land of that rough country it runs straight and determined, often in the

The empress Helena, associated in the myth with Macsen but in fact the mother of Constantine the Great, had coins minted with her image.

Walls of the Roman fort's outpost still stand to some height outside Caernarfon.

form of a track across the moorland, wide enough still to take a vehicle, probably there for ever.

It is the density of its association with myth that make Segontium remarkable among archeological sites. Moreover it and the tale together illustrate powerfully the way myth works. It selects fragments of differing sorts of reality and renders them symbolic. The process which happened to Magnus Maximus might well be that which happened to the original of King Arthur, or, come to that, the original of Agamemnon, or Moses, or even Christ. The crystallisation of a whole succession of events — the coming of the Romans, their liaison with the island's natives, connections of Emperors with Britain, the building of forts and roads, the eventual withdrawal and the role played in that by Maximus — into a single story, also provides a fine example of a process often achieved by myth, in which, for instance, many tribal feuds may be represented as a single battle, or many floods become summarised as one great Flood.

Sarn Helen, one of the roads called after Elen, or Helena, can still be clearly seen running across the moorland above the Lledr valley (above) and behind Trawsfynydd (below).

The Saxons Arrive

The early history of this island is a catalogue of invasions. Indeed the history of islands usually is, and all that is remarkable about ours is that they stopped. In remembering that we have not been invaded since 1066, we easily forget that what was invaded then was an amalgam of several thousand years of successive invasions. The Normans simply added a veneer to a lamination which included equivalent layers of pre-Celtic cairn-builders and pre-Bronze Age cromlech-builders.

It is odd that the island now is generally thought of as England, since that place, Angle-land, never really existed. Certainly the Mercians and Northumbrians, two occasionally powerful groups in a country also occupied by West Saxons, Middle and South Saxons, Jutes, Picts, and various tribes of Britons, were indeed originally Angles, but they never entirely unified the country, which for several hundred years was in a state of constant war. Alfred the Great styled himself 'King of all England', even though he was a West Saxon; but within a little more than a hundred years of his death in 899 the country was largely ruled by Danes, and it was indeed a Danish king of 'England', Harold II, who was defeated at the Battle of Hastings, in October, 1066. After that the country would have been more appropriately called New Normandy.

There is no doubt however that at some early point in that development a recognisable change had occurred, and this is once again summarised for us in the form of strong and simple images by the mythology. It was not of course the simple set of occurrences by which myth, and indeed early history, remembers it. Known as the 'adventus Saxonum', this is largely the invention of Bede, the founder of our formal written history, but he derived it from earlier sources, notably Gildas and the 'Historia Brittonum', a collection made from much older material by a North Wales priest called Nennius, in about 800 AD. From these origins the material passed through a familiar expansion in the imagination of Geoffrey of

Monmouth, and interestingly a related but apparently independent Welsh tale gives us another view of the same subject.

Geoffrey took from Nennius the simple but compelling episode in which the Saxons and the Britons come to a meeting to discuss the terms of a truce, the former however bringing with them daggers concealed in their boots, the latter attending unarmed. The native British High-king Vortigern survived that archetypal event, still known to us as the Night of the Long Knives. Moving further from history into myth, Nennius takes us straight from that slaughter into Snowdonia.

The retreating king made for the fastnesses of North Wales, that bulk of scrub and crag which was to be the last-stand refuge for later independent princes too, and there, under Snowdon, he tried to build a castle. As much as he built during the day, however, disappeared during the night. The king consulted his wise men — an implication, perhaps, of the heathen, perhaps Druidic surroundings of the story — who directed him to sacrifice on the spot a boy without a father. This too takes us back to pre-history, being some confirmation of the Romans' accusation that the Druids practised human sacrifice; and the demand that it should be a child may be connected with the discovery by modern archeology of the buried bones of children in connection with stone circles, such as that known as the Druids' Circle above Penmaenmawr.

In any case we are suddenly into myth, the world of apparent impossibility. Themes such as negociating with invaders fade away, and the mystery of supernatural conception and the ritual of child-sacrifice replace them.

Messengers, the Nennius story continues, were sent out. In the south of Wales they eventually found a boy who claimed to have no father, and they brought him north to Snowdon. Confronted on the hilltop below the mountain by Vortigern and his advisers, and by imminent death, he demanded to question the wise men. The important events which then took place, and the long background to them in myth and history, will concern us again, in Chapter Six

Dinas Emrys, a hill below Snowdon at the head of Nantgwynant, is the focal point of the stories of Vortigern and Emrys.

of this book. Here we must follow the fate of Vortigern, represented as the last High-king of pre-Saxon Britain.

Having outwitted the wise men, by, as we shall see, displaying greater knowledge than theirs, the boy gave his name: Ambros. The hill, he said, would thenceforth be his, and indeed it is still known as Dinas Emrys.

There can be no doubt that the character in this tale refers to someone who actually existed. In the early Welsh literature he appears as Emrys, and this, it is clear, is the name given in these versions to the most notable and respected of the British leaders of the early post-Roman period, Ambrosius Aurelianus.

Although in many respects biased, the historian Gildas sees very clearly the historical causes of the turmoil of his time, the mid-sixth century. Ambrosius emerges as the hero partly because of Gildas' concerns, since Gildas was focussing on Vortigern's inadequacy and its consequences. As a cleric he was perhaps more naturally inclined to the Romanised, civilised and ordered world which

Now illegible, the Eliseg pillar's inscription once carried a reference to Vortigern.

Ambrosius, with his Roman name, seemed to him to stand for. We detect in the myth, at any rate, vestiges of pagan influences shadowing the character of Vortigern. He was, it seems, representative of the fragmentation, the decay of political administration, which for a time replaced all that Gildas admired.

'Tunc omnes consiliarii una cum superbo tyrano caecantur adinvenientes tal praesidium . . .' 'All the counsellors and the high and mighty king were blinded then, such defence did they devise.' The anger in his voice is still clear to us more than fourteen centuries later; and indeed those events which brought Ambrosius and Vortigern to that hilltop in the myth have results for us too. They spawned a very long descent of disordering effects. What, then, is the background to this strange and crucial North Wales encounter?

Vortigern, it seems, was having trouble controlling the extremities of his kingdom. He engaged Saxon troops to act as mercenaries, to combat what Gildas describes as the northern nations, presumably the Picts and the Scots. Britain apparently still suffered from a lack of fighting forces, though if we follow the dating which Bede drew from Gildas and place Vortigern's problem at around 446 AD, some sixty years have elapsed since the mass exodus under Macsen. It seems that at first the ploy was successful; the Saxons did their job well; but Gildas, with the advantage of hindsight, pinpoints the error as allowing them into the island at all, 'like wolves into folds'.

Evidently the immigrants liked the look of the country which they found, and recognised its potential. They soon sent for their families and friends, and their numbers quickly became larger than Vortigern and his advisers had bargained for. They then broke the treaty on the pretext that the supplies with which they were paid were insufficient, allied themselves to the Picts whom they had been fighting, and laid waste the land 'from sea to sea'. Vortigern fled to North Wales.

Archeology indicates in fact that by 450 there had been settled groups of Saxons in Britain for some time. Germanic troops fought in the Roman army, for instance defending the Wall against the

Nant Gwrtheyrn, last hiding place of Vortigern, is a sheer and inaccessible valley.

Picts, foreshadowing Vortigern's use of their compatriots for the same purpose.

Vortigern himself has some historical authenticity, although the word is probably a title rather than a personal name, in the same way as Caesar. He turns up again in an early ninth century inscription on a pillar at Valle Crucis Abbey, just outside Llangollen, where he is named as the son-in-law of Maximus himself, the hero of our previous chapter. This however represents the geneological claims of a prince of Powys, so that we must take it as rather an indication of who was thought to be historically important in the ninth century, and not reliable evidence of Vortigern's actual position in British history.

His name, however, is remembered in topography around North Wales, indicating that he had some special connection with the area. Most notably a tradition locates his next place of refuge. Handing over Dinas Emrys to its new lord, 'Ambros', he retreated to the Lleyn peninsula. There a valley is still called after him Nant Gwrtheyrn, 'Vortigern's valley'.

By any standards Nant Gwrtheyrn is a strange place. Enclosed on all sides by sheer slopes, it is something like a vast ravine. If protection was his requirement, Vortigern found it. Nant Gwrtheyrn is definitively isolated. No wonder it has been a place of refuge, evidently, for some considerable time. The valley is dotted with hut circles and early long-huts, and the mound called Castell Gwrtheyrn, 'Vortigern's castle', was the site of a burial chamber visible until the late 18th century, when the local people opened it and found there, so we are told, the bones of a tall man buried in a stone coffin. Now, with unusual appropriateness, this place so poignantly associated with the nation's past is the home of the National Language School, a centre for the teaching of the Welsh language.

The Collapse of the Celtic Kingdoms

On an island in the middle of what is now known as Bala lake there lived a man called Tegid Foel, together with his wife and two children. This was, however, no ordinary family, but rather one of the great families in Celtic myth. The wife was the goddess Ceridwen, muse-goddess, goddess of knowledge and inspiration. They had two children, remarkable for the fact that one of them was the most beautiful girl in the world, the other, with the appropriately unpleasant name of Afagddu, the ugliest boy.

There is evidently no problem about being the most beautiful girl in the world, and accordingly we hear no more about the daughter. Afagddu however caused his loving mother some heartache. Wisdom is some compensation for lack of beauty, and so she determined to provide him with supreme wisdom as a balance to his supreme ugliness. Using a recipe she had found in an ancient book (probably a reference to some mystical classical text) she set about boiling up the broth of knowledge and inspiration.

The cauldron she used for the purpose had to be on the boil for a year and a day. It has, in a way, been boiling ever since, in the form of alchemists' vessels, of witches' cauldrons, and of many other sacramental vessels, including the Christian chalice, which promise to provide some element missing in our mortality — supreme knowledge, power, or eternal life. It is among other things one of the prototypes of the Holy Grail, which we shall be considering again in Chapter Seven of this book.

Ceridwen's concoction consisted of herbs which she gathered and cast into the cauldron at the right state of the stars. This suggests that the sort of knowledge it was to produce was astrological, and the year-and-a-day prescription would enable the completion of all possible cycles, on the earth and in its relation to the solar system. The story concerns us here, however, not so much for its mystical connections but because it provides the base from which a great myth-cycle is launched into the mainstream of British tradition.

The main protagonist of the tale is not the hapless Afagddu, who indeed gets no further mention. Ceridwen set a blind man and a boy to kindle the fire and stir the cauldron, while she was presumably off herb-gathering. It is the boy, Gwion bach, who becomes the focus of our tale. Towards the end of the period the mixture had become reduced to three drops, and these accidentally flew out of the cauldron and landed on Gwion's finger. 'And by reason of their great heat he put his finger to his mouth,' and at once knew everything, including what was about to happen. One thing that was about to happen was that Ceridwen was going to try to destroy him, and he took rather urgent evasive action.

A shape-shifting sequence then follows, in which he turns into a hare, she into a greyhound, he into a fish, she into an otter, he into a bird, she into a hawk, and finally, finding a barn, he hides himself as a grain in a heap of wheat. There is, however, no avoiding destiny. Ceridwen enters the barn in the form of a black hen, picks out the grain which is Gwion, and swallows him.

The transformation process is familiar, a common theme in Celtic myth, and may be something to do with the roles of the Celtic gods in nature, or, more probably, with the belief in metempsychosis which Caesar recorded as being a chief belief of the Druids. In any case the image of rebirth is explicit here, since Ceridwen on her return to human form finds herself pregnant by the seed which she has swallowed, and in due course Gwion is born again.

Many heroes have to undergo an apparent death and rebirth before they can take up their individual function. When Gwion was born again he was subjected to a further trial, since Ceridwen, now unwilling to destroy him, set him to sea in a sewn-up basket, just as Perseus was set adrift in Greek myth, Moses in Judaic, and so on. Like so many other heroes Gwion survived this almost certain death, and like them too he was found and fostered by a prince.

Gwion was found washed up in a weir in the south of North Wales ('between Dyfi and Aberystwyth') which was the property of a king called Gwyddno, and which was fished by his son Elffin, a prince remarkable for his ill fortune. Though the weir was

The witch-goddess Ceridwen lived with her husband Tegid Foel on an island in the middle of Bala lake.

normally abundant with salmon, since Elffin had been fishing it there had been nothing, except now this leather-wrapped basket. What he found within it, however, to some extent reversed Elffin's habitual bad luck.

Tradition, and one of the Welsh 'Triads', interjects into the story of Elffin son of Gwyddno an element which does not occur in the main written versions. Gwyddno's kingdom was low lying and coastal, and therefore protected from the sea by an embankment. The Triad blames the drunkeness of Seithennyn (who evidently was in charge of the sea-defences) for letting the land become submerged. In one great storm the whole country, which is said to have contained sixteen fortified towns, was lost, and the inhabitants who escaped retreated to live in the uplands.

Clearly this episode has elements in it which are more than mere folk-tale, related as it is to the universal myths of floods and inundations, the theme exemplified by the Noah story and the tale of Atlantis. There are other examples even within British myth, notably the lost land of Lyonesse. Golden and idyllic, these places lie with their great civilised cities, their rich lands and lovely palaces, lost for ever below the unrevealing sea. The theme in myth as usual serves several purposes. It reflects a memory of coastal changes, of real rises in sea level or sinking of the land in perhaps countless past times. Such things do happen, as one can see for oneself from the drowned forests of our low-tide beaches and the engulfed churchyards of our shores. Also of course the image acts as a metaphor for the past itself, golden in memory, rich and secure and with a kinder climate, which has, as if submerged by a relentless tide, irretrievably gone.

Like many such notions this one claims a factual as well as a symbolic truth. Gwyddno's kingdom is believed still to obtrude above the surface of the lowest tides of Cardigan Bay, in the form of a long, dark line of stones, running at right angles to the coastline out to sea, where it continues for some fourteen miles. The local strength of the story has proved resilient in the face of a complete lack of evidence that this line of stones is artificial.

The reef, known as Sarn Badrig, 'St Patrick's causeway', is

The remarkable reef called Sarn Badrig is said to be the remains of the sea defences of the drowned land of Cantre'r Gwælod.

visible off the coast about halfway between Harlech and Barmouth. It starts about a mile from the coastline, and runs in a south-west direction. The connection with St Patrick comes from another tradition, to the effect that the saint crossed by it from Wales to Ireland. Undeniably it is unusually straight for any natural object, and the idea will not die that this is all that is left of Gwyddno's kingdom, Cantre'r Gwaelod, the 'bottom hundred'.

All this, then, lay in Elffin's past, as, bereft of his inheritance, he fished the weir near Aberdyfi. Finding the bag which contained the reborn Gwion, he renamed him (because of his 'radiant brow') Taliesin. The story in effect says that the great prophet-bard gained his mystical knowledge because in a previous life he had drunk of Ceridwen's cauldron.

Taliesin is both a figure of early history, (a Dark Age poet associated with Urien of Rheged, a northern British king), and a looming mystic and magician not unlike the early forms of Merlin. In his historical form he wrote dense, aphoristic verse, some of which still survives — although much has been attributed to him in the past which was probably by his contemporaries or by later writers. As a figure of myth he forms the central role in one extraordinary North Wales story.

Elffin, we are told, besides being the son of King Gwyddno, was the nephew of the king of Gwynedd, a little further north. King Maelgwn ruled Gwynedd from his citadel-fort at Deganwy, overlooking the Conwy river. It was to that luxurious court that Elffin came on a visit.

Maelgwn appears in the story as a quick-tempered and high-handed ruler, surrounded by flattering courtiers and bards whose job it is to recite his praise. It is partly because of this desperate need for eulogy that uncle and nephew fall out. Elffin has the audacity to claim that his wife is as faithful as Maelgwn's and his bard as skilful. A strong folk-tale element enters in the next sequence with the testing of the fidelity of his wife, but immediately after that the tale gets on with its main subject, and strikes a more symbolic note again with the entry of Taliesin, now Elffin's personal bard.

The Vardre, above Deganwy, was the seat of the historical king Maelgwn Gwynedd, who reigned in the sixth century and who features in the mythology as the uncle of Elffin.

Taliesin, it appears, has taken skill as a bard to its ultimate length; with him poetry has become spell, and he uses it to work magic. First he now spellbinds Maelgwn's flattering bards, so that all they can do is make a bubbling noise with their fingers on their lips, which the tale attractively represents as 'blerwm blerwm'. When asked by Maelgwn who he is, he launches into a long and awe-inspiring riddle:

> I was with my lord in the heavens
> When Lucifer fell into the depth of hell.
> I carried a banner in front of Alexander . . .
> I brought seed down to the vale of Hebron;
> I was in the court of Don before the birth of Gwydion;
> I was patriarch to Elijah and Enoch . . .

A long list of Old Testament and British references, intermingled, follows, until it is clear that what he is saying is that he is the timeless world-spirit, present everywhere on all occasions, no less at the birth of Christ than in the prison of Arianrhod. He also mentions his present incarnation and its immediate prelude: 'I obtained inspiration from the cauldron of Ceridwen'; and he ends by answering the question in the sense in which it was asked:

> Then for nine months I was
> In the womb of the witch Ceridwen;
> I was formerly little Gwion;
> And now I am Taliesin.

He then sang other verses, the effect of which was to raise such a storm over that hilltop castle at Deganwy that the king was afraid that the perilously perched towers would fall around them; he released Elffin from the prison into which he had impetuously thrown him, and Taliesin broke his fetters off with another spell.

It is at this stage in the story that the texts introduce the prophecies. In effect, he foretells the loss of Britain to the Saxons:

A coiling serpent,
Proud and merciless,
With golden wings,
 Out of Germany.

It shall overrun
Lloegyr and Scotland,
From the Scandinavian Sea,
 To the river Severn.

Then will the Britons be
Like prisoners,
Exiled from their rights
 By Saxony.

Yet not quite the whole of the country was to be lost. There follows then the verse which has given us, through George Borrows' fortunate use of its last line, a phrase which now comes naturally to describe the land left to these new exiles:

They shall praise their lord,
And they shall keep their language;
Their land they shall lose,
 Except wild Wales.

These sentiments would probably have puzzled Maelgwn, distant from the invasions in his western citadel and surrounded by his yes-men. No doubt this 'prophecy', like most, was composed with the benefit of hindsight, which is why it seems to us so accurate. That too is part of the function of myth, to look back and express what the people in the past should have seen, but failed to, what they could have avoided had they understood their situation properly. The story, including the poems, occurs in the Red Book of Hergest, a manuscript of the late fourteenth or early fifteenth century, although no doubt it is a transcription of older traditional material.

Other prophecies are attributed to Taliesin at this juncture, but these occur only in later versions, as does the story of the various exploits of Maelgwn and his death. In spite of this slight doubt as to their antiquity, some of these do seem to refer to authentically traditional material. The prophesied death of Maelgwn is a particularly deserving case, since it echoes the prophecies made of the death of kings in other mythologies, particularly in the Irish tales. Once foretold, such a death is unavoidable, and although Maelgwn attempts to hide from it this is in vain.

Taliesin foretold that a yellow monster would come out of the plain of Rhianedd to destroy him:

> E ddaw pryf rhyfedd
> O Forfa Rhianedd
> I ddial anwiredd
> Ar Faelgwn Gwynedd;
> A'i flew a'i ddannedd
> A'i lygaid yn euredd,
> A hyn a wna ddiwedd
> Ar Faelgwn Gwynedd.

Morfa Rhianedd, '*the plain of Rhianedd*', was probably a large area of marsh and sand-dunes including both the area where Llandudno now stands and that stretch of bay supposed once to have been dry land, the lost kingdom of Llys Helig, between the Great Orme and Penmaenmawr. The king was so fearful of the coming of the monster which was to destroy him that he took refuge in the little church of Llanrhos nearby. The tale tells that he was unable to control his curiosity and looked out through the keyhole. One glimpse of the monster approaching was enough to kill him.

St Hilary's church at Llanrhos is today a solid stone building of largely 13th century date, so that it was not through this particular keyhole that the old king looked. However it is likely that in this case as in so many the building stands on the site of a 6th century foundation, an early religious cell originally made of wood and

Maelgwn is said in the story to have died in the church at Llanrhos, in hiding from the yellow monster.

The plain of Morfa Rhianedd, from which the monster came which killed King Maelgwn, was the plain on which the town of Llandudno stands and at one time extended into Conwy Bay.

wattle. There is a tradition that King Maelgwn was buried under the south door, although other traditions site his burial on Puffin Island and elsewhere. The wooded hill beyond the church is still called after him, Bryn Maelgwyn (as his name is spelt in anglicised form), and indeed he is commemorated in the area in a wide variety of forms, some of which (such as the local telephone exchange) would certainly have surprised him.

The yellow monster of the prophecy and story seems to bear several references, since it cannot but be reminiscent of the yellow dragon mentioned by both Taliesin and (as we shall see in Chapter Six) by his fellow-prophet Merlin. To them it undoubtedly stood for the invading Anglo-Saxons. However it is traditionally equated historically with the Yellow Plague, and the Welsh Annals (which may date originally from the years they refer to) provide some corrobation for this. They give, for the year 547, the summary 'an. mortalitas magna in qua pausat Mailcun rex Guenedotiae' — 'a year of great death in which Maelgwn king of Gwynedd died'. We know from other sources that the Yellow Plague had spread across Europe from the Middle East during the previous five years, and swept through Britain towards the end of the 540's. We also gather from the Welsh poems 'The Stanzas of the Graves' (which occur in a twelfth century manuscript but again are clearly a medium for remembering events of very early history as well as various heroic traditions) that the plain of Rhianedd was a place of burials, and one of the Triads gives as the origin of the plague in Gwynedd the corpses left there after a battle.

We gain from the historian Gildas, his contemporary, some knowledge of the historical Maelgwn, king of Gwynedd. We are told that his life was one of constant quarrelling, with his family, with the church, with other kings. Besides less dreadful crimes he had his wife removed and married the wife of his nephew — the basis, perhaps, of the quarrel with Elffin in the story. Gildas is specific about him: "When it is possible to catch your attention it is not hymns you want to hear, the praises of God, but your own praises, uttered by that set of lying rascals." Gildas points to the behaviour of kings such as Maelgwn as the root of the decline of

The name of Maelgwn is still in use in the neighbourhood in which he once reigned.

Britain in the post-Roman period. The great cities of Britain lie neglected, "because, although wars with foreigners have ceased, domestic wars continue".

Archeologically too the number and size of the courts of post-Roman Britain indicates such a disunity. The archeology also indicates, ironically, that this period of political decline was a time of wealth.

That this hilltop above Deganwy was occupied by a court of some luxury at about the time of Maelgwn has been proved, by excavations carried out by Leslie Alcock in the 1960's. The crucial evidence of its status consists of some pieces of Mediterranean pottery wine-jars, and although the quantity is insufficient to suggest a well-stocked cellar, the conclusion does seem to follow that a king who could afford imported wines was in the élite class of his time.

It is perhaps the two tales in combination, representing as they do losses of land, and the ending of better times, which embody the memory of the loss of Britain which Gildas and others record. Gwyddno suffered the disaster of the flooding of the best part of his land; Maelgwn, taunted with his failure by Taliesin, lost his people, his kingdom, and his life. Preoccupied with their personal tragedies and quarrels, the kings who could have unified to resist the invasions of Britain instead turned their minds away from the real dangers (hinted at by Taliesin) which were looming on their eastern horizons.

Only fragments remain of the several castles which stood on the hilltop of the Vardre.

Merlin at Dinas Emrys

The unfolding story of Merlin in British myth takes us from the pre-Roman, independent period, through the Roman occupation, into the Dark Ages and the early Middle Ages, and towards the re-emergence of national identity and pride. Much of this takes place in a complex of stories set in North Wales.

We have mentioned the hill in Snowdonia, Dinas Emrys, before, in Chapter Four, in connection with the flight of Vortigern after his betrayal by the Saxons. Vortigern's wise men had told him that to succeed in building his citadel he must sacrifice on the spot a boy without a father. Such a boy had in due course been found, and brought to the hilltop. He then asked to be allowed to question the wise men, and subsequently displayed greater knowledge than them. What was it, he asked, that was hidden under the paving on the hill's summit? They did not know, but he did. There was a pool there. They opened the paving, and found the pool. To their ignorance he replied that there were two containers; on separating the containers they would find a wrapping — literally a 'tent' between two 'vases'; and in the wrapping two serpents, one of them white, the other red. All this was discovered as predicted, and when they then unfolded the cloth and released the serpents he told them also what would happen next. The serpents began to fight each other, the white one at first winning, and then, after the third near defeat, the red one recovering and finally driving out the white. The king and his magicians stood astonished as the prophetic boy explained all this to them. The pool, he told them, was the world, the tent Vortigern's kingdom. The two serpents were the dragons of two nations, the red one that of the natives of Britain, the white one the invading Saxons. In the end, he said, our people will drive out the Saxons and send them back to where they came from. But as far as Vortigern was concerned, there was no future for him on this hill. It was he, the boy, who should have control of the castle to be built there. He gave his name then: Ambros.

On the summit of Dinas Emrys is a marshy hollow, conforming to the spot in the story where Emrys released the fighting dragons.

The view from the top of Dinas Emrys.

In his great compilation, 'The History of the Kings of Britain', Geoffrey of Monmouth lifted, almost intact, the Ambros-Emrys story from the early historian Nennius. His purpose, however, was to pull together the various strands of authentic national mythical material which had survived down to his time. One set of these concerned a character called Myrddin, whose origins appear to lie in North Britain where he was a sixth century poet, contemporary of Taliesin. Legends had begun to cluster around him, and Geoffrey built on these. His long and rambling book has several prominent heroes, the greatest among them being Arthur. As the expression of a less militaristic, less political aspect of national identity he needed a figure of mystery and power, representative of that under-current of authentic early British tradition.

The Myrddin of the tradition current in his time was just such a figure. He came out of the depths of ancient British thought as if out of a dark forest. The hilltop confrontation of Emrys and Vortigern provided the setting for the proclamation of a national prophecy, and Geoffrey, by placing the seer Myrddin in the position of the prophetic boy Emrys, brought into being a new amalgam which, although it was his own invention, had such strong dual roots in native British myth that Merlin has survived as perhaps the best-known and the most impressive native mythic figure after Arthur.

Merlin has several strands of origin, but this combination of Geoffrey's and the location in North Wales of the Nennius story pinpoint the Snowdonian hilltop still called Dinas Emrys as the place at which he came into being. Why, one wonders, should it have been here? What was it about Dinas Emrys which picked it out for this important role in myth?

Dinas Emrys stands in mountain country, so close under the shoulder of Snowdon itself that the bulk of the mountain is hidden from there by its own expanding flanks. Snowdon is a presence above, indicated by the jut of the boulders and the rearing horizons of heather. The valley curves towards Dinas Emrys under Snowdon's broader extremities, and over it stands this small, round hill, its natural cragginess blurred by its clothing of brown scrub oak, like ivy on a castle ruin.

The joining-points of any diverse elements have an intrinsic fascination, as if one can still not quite believe that it can at one and the same time be day and night. Myth often occurs in such a half-light, and perhaps not a little of its appeal lies in its ill-defined, ambiguous relationship to history. All the more intriguing is it when the overlap occurs at an identifiable place, as we may see it do again in other chapters. Here on the round, flat summit of Dinas Emrys, overlooking the Gwynant valley and Llyn Dinas, the clustering of ideas and themes from these different, and distant, regions is almost overwhelming.

'Dinas', though it means 'city' in Welsh, is a word often given to ancient fortified settlements, and so might best be translated 'fortress'. Defensive structures have indeed been found there, in the course of excavations carried out in the mid-1950's. A castle was built on the top of the hill as late as the twelfth century, and the square base of this medieval tower is still clearly visible (though nothing further is known of it than its date and its existence), providing evidence that somebody was here during the century in which Geoffrey of Monmouth was writing. That old ruin, it turns out, is simply the last period of the place's inhabitation. As early as the Roman age, perhaps before, the hill was occupied. The finds — sherds, amphorae, and ornaments — indicate a court of some luxury there towards the end of the fifth century, the time, that is, of Ambrosius, immediately after the traditional date of Vortigern and the Saxon invasion. An even more remarkable connection, however, between archeology and myth, was the opening up of a concealed pool, just such as that described by the myth in which the two serpents were, it tells us, buried.

In the centre of the summit plateau of Dinas Emrys is a deep hollow, almost a glade, boggy and tangled with clumps of reed. During the excavations, a square depression in this miniature marshy valley was found to be a man-made pool, a cistern, probably cut during the early-Roman period of the hill's occupation; pre-Ambrosius, pre-Vortigern, and certainly long pre-Nennius. On the banks of this pool and over an area of the pool where it had silted, a paved stone platform was discovered, thought, this time, to belong to the Dark Age period. Under the circumstances one can hardly resist the speculation that the paving would have covered the whole pool and the rest of it had been removed by Vortigern's magicians in their earlier excavations carried out under the direction of Emrys-Merlin.

They however, though not the last to dig there, were, the myth tells us, not the first either. A story in the Mabinogion, 'Lludd and Llefelys', tells, among other events, how the dragon-serpents came to be there, and in doing so it curiously anticipates the early-Roman dating of the cistern. Though, in the form in which we have it, the story dates from the fourteenth century, and might therefore be nothing more than a conscious addition to the Geoffrey of Monmouth story, it is generally agreed that, like much of the Mabinogion, it was very probably based on much older original material — though the age of the source material is debated, and probably undiscoverable. Since episodes of the Welsh story occur in Welsh translations of Geoffrey but not, unlike the start of the story, in the original Latin version, it seems probable that both Geoffrey and the compiler of the Mabinogion tale were working from some old traditional source. If so, the later story seems to imply that the Merlin figure knew the earlier story of the burial of the dragons and used it, perhaps, to tap the spirit of nationalism by evoking traditional myth. That is, Emrys-Merlin knew from 'Lludd and Llefelys' not only what was buried on Dinas Emrys, but the significance of it. Certainly the story of Lludd and Llefelys, with its world of magic and enchantment and its primitive imagery, feels the older of the two. Certainly too it seems to have deeper roots in British myth.

Lludd's otherwise fortunate rule over Britain was disturbed by three plagues. The first was an invading nation with super-natural gifts, who could hear anything that was said, no matter how quietly it was spoken; and by this talent they avoided attack. The second plague was a scream which happened everywhere in the country every May-eve, terrifying the population and causing barrenness.

The third plague was the disappearance of all the food prepared in the king's court which was not consumed on the first night.

Lludd sought the advice of his brother Llefelys, by then king of France. The first plague was dealt with, after some set-backs, by sprinkling a magic potion over all the people, which poisoned the foreigners but left one's own folk unharmed. The third plague was revealed to be a giant, who carried away the food and drink, and this was solved by lying in wait and overcoming him. These are easy enough solutions, but it is the way the remaining plague, the second one, is dealt with which concerns us here.

Llefelys explained it to Lludd. What is causing the omnipresent scream is the battling of two dragons. The dragon of a foreign nation is struggling to overcome the native dragon, which, on the point of defeat, utters the scream. In the centre of the country Lludd was to place a tub of mead, in a pit, covered over with a silk cloth. The dragons would come to rest on the cloth, sink into the mead, drink it, and sleep. They were then to be wrapped up in the covering, sealed in a stone chest, and buried in the ground in the strongest place the king could find in his dominions. 'And as long as they stay in that secure place, no plague will come to Britain from elsewhere.' In other words, as in the case which we shall later encounter of Brân's severed head, they were to be a safeguard against invasion. Is the imagery making a reference, perhaps forgotten or no longer understood, to a decision to stop resisting the Romans and instead allow them to take up the role of protectors? Like all true symbolism, these dragons are suggestive but obscure.

Lludd did as he was instructed, and in due course the dragons came, fought, fell asleep, were wrapped and enclosed in their stone jar. 'And in the safest place he found in Snowdonia he hid them. And after that the place was called Dinas Emrys.'

Lludd in the story was one of the sons of Beli the Great — and that, the opening statement, connects him at once with Britain at the time of the Roman invasion. It was from Beli that Macsen took the island of Britain, when he came as Emperor of Rome with his followers in search of his dream-love. We may therefore safely regard Lludd as a figure connected with the coming of the Romans, and thought of as ruling Britain either before or during the early-Roman period. The name itself comes from that of a Celtic deity, since he is the same person as Nudd, or in Irish Nuadha, known to the Romans and Romanised Celts as Nodens. It was to Nodens that the fourth century temple at Lydney in Gloucestershire was dedicated, and though the date of this makes it more an instance of a late revival of the Romano Celtic merging of religion than an authentic piece of evidence — and is thought, anyway, to indicate rather an Irish colonisation than an indigenous cult — it does at least imply that Nodens, or Nudd, or Lludd, was a highly respected deity.

In the story, however, we see more of a historicised being, a king of Britain who built cities. As such he has a rich enough set of offshoots and effects in the mythology, since in the confusion of the pedigrees in another Mabinogion story he is given a daughter called Creiddylad, who, as the origin of Cordelia, makes him one of the origins of King Lear. He also has another notable achievement to his credit, since both Geoffrey and the Mabinogion, in an identical passage, attribute to him the establishing of the city of London. In making it his capital he encouraged the building there of houses of a splendour never before seen. So great was his effect on it that it was named after him, Caer Lludd, or, as it became, Caer Lundein. Lludd-din, perhaps, Lludd's city? Hence, in Roman times, Londinium. In later ages, in any case, Lludd was not forgotten there, and indeed, as King Lud, is still remembered; one of the gates, as Geoffrey puts it, 'in the British tongue is still called Porthlud after him, although in Saxon it bears the name Ludgate'. Perhaps the gate got its name originally by its proximity to a temple dedicated to Lud's original, the god from whom he has become historicised. Interestingly Geoffrey also says that the city has another gate which is called Billingsgate after Beli, whom he calls Belinus, thus bringing together again the father and son of this early British myth.

Since the Lludd story specifies that the country was to be safe from invasion as long as the dragons were still buried, it seems that by instructing Vortigern's magicians to unearth them Ambros-Merlin was (by a sort of inversion of cause and effect) accepting that the Saxon invasion had taken place. Perhaps the story implies that he, unlike Vortigern, saw that it was necessary to fight, rather than run away: letting loose the dragons certainly had the effect of setting them warring again. After the easy acceptance of life under the Romans it was perhaps a significant change; and although the invading dragon appeared to be winning, the prophet's message was that the spirit of national resistance would in the end dominate. Similarly the Ambrosius of history seems to have stirred and drawn together the remnants of native British independence. Perhaps the myth recognises in this some permanent achievement. Perhaps by refusing to take the Saxon invasion in a spirit of retreat Ambrosius made possible not only the Arthurian resistance but even the continuing existence of identifiable Celtic regions today. Wales and Cornwall, at least, did survive.

The symbolism too remains with us. There was a sense in which the red dragon did literally make its prophesied come-back. Probably the original story drew its imagery from an early Welsh custom of going into battle under the standard of a dragon of an identifying colour, and if so it was simply in continuation of this tradition that Henry Tudor bore that emblem on one of his banners at the Battle of Bosworth. The figure of the red dragon on a green and white background went back to the seventh century Welsh king Cadwaladr, from whom the Anglesey family of Tudor claimed descent, so that it was, in effect, one of Henry's family devices. It had long before been recognised as representing Wales; the Welsh troops of the Black Prince, for instance, threw such a banner over him as Prince of Wales, when he fell from his horse at the battle of Crecy.

Henry Tudor's flying of the Red Dragon on the field of Bosworth, may well have indicated a knowledge of the Merlin story and the prophesy on Dinas Emrys, and certainly it showed a recognition of the latent power of native British nationalism, even at that relatively late date. He presented himself to the people as

Welsh, landed in Wales, and marched through South Wales to the border collecting support. A bardic prophecy of the time actually referred to him as a dragon, of the blood of the ancient British lineage, 'the hope of our race'. Dinas Emrys had not been forgotten, and in a sense Merlin's prophecy came partly true, in the August of 1485.

For one hilltop to be associated with so potent a symbol as the red dragon, and, at the same time, so impressive a figure as Merlin, is in itself remarkable. That it should also be the spot connected in myth with the first stages of the Saxon invasion of Britain, and thus form a junction of the streams of myth, history, and archeology, is perhaps a little too much to assimilate. It is, after all, an unassuming hill, looking out onto the soft peace of Llyn Dinas. What the myth says and the hill embodies is that the most ancient aspects of native British identity survived intact through great cultural changes by being protected from change by the harsh terrain of the hills. Anywhere so clearly characterised as wild and inaccessible had a role to play both in history and in the national thinking. It is because of that that the myth which summarises the first disruptions caused by the arrival of the Saxons sees Vortigern, as high-king, retreating to the same place as that in which Lludd dealt with, apparently, the earlier invasion of the Romans. What better place for Emrys to rally the spirit of native resistance, than out on that crag under the side of Snowdon.

Indeed, not much changes here. From the top of Snowdon on a winter evening one still sees a raw country, a bare spread of rock-ridges and spurs, the pale icing of frost and hail whitening their tops, their sides black with wet cliffs. It expands in a sweep of ranges northwards, rearing and rolling in much the same conformation as they did a few million years ago when the ice slid off them.

HARRI TUDUR

DIEV·ET·MON·

DROYT·

The symbolism of the dragon story of Dinas Emrys developed into the emblem of Wales, the red dragon of its early kings and of its present flag.

Brân and the Holy Grail

Mystic vessels with supernatural powers occur early in our native mythology. We have already encountered one, in Chapter Five: the cauldron of inspiration, in which the witch-goddess Ceridwen boiled up the concoction which was to make her ugly son all-knowing. That was one of the basic roots of the Holy Grail. Another is the cauldron of rebirth.

The Mabinogion story 'Branwen, daughter of Llŷr' is not a happy one. It concerns the unsuccessful marriage of Branwen to the king of Ireland. At the beginning of the story Brân, king of the Island of Britain, is sitting with his brother Manawydan on the rock of Harlech, where the famous castle now stands, looking out to sea. The ships of the king of Ireland come towards them, and on enquiring they discover his mission. He has come to ask for the hand of Brân's sister, Branwen. A marriage is arranged to take place at the court of Aberffraw, in Anglesey (in historical times one of the seats of the kings of Gwynedd, later of the princes of North Wales). Some trouble ensues, and it becomes necessary to placate the Irish king. For this purpose Brân decides to present him with the most precious thing he has, which is a cauldron with a magic property of some worth. It will restore the dead to life.

The trouble, however, continues between the two kingdoms — a reflection, probably, of the constant problem of invasion from Ireland from early times, as evidenced by archeology, by place names, and by early tradition. Humiliated by her husband, Branwen sends a secret message to Brân, by means of training a starling to convey it, all communication between Britain and Ireland by then being cut off. The starling found him at 'Caer Seint in Arfon', in other words at Segontium, the site of the story which we told in Chapter Three. Brân at once gathers his men and sets off for Ireland. In those days, we are told, the channel was not so wide — no doubt a reference to the inundations of the kingdoms of the coastline, such as Cantre'r Gwaelod — and he himself, evidently of

Brân looked out to sea from the rock of Harlech, where the medieval castle now stands.

In the story Brân held court at Aberffraw, in history one of the courts of the princes of Gwynedd.

gigantic size, went across by wading. He was too big, the tale adds, to be contained in a ship.

After some parleying and some trickery, a battle ensues. The Irish make good use of their secret weapon. All the dead warriors are put each night to boil in the cauldron of rebirth, and in the morning they are back on the job.

The idea, as one would expect, is not new. Something of the sort seems to be indicated by the Greek story of Medea, another enchantress who possessed a cauldron, who promised the daughters of Peleus renewed youth for their father, and with that ostensible aim got them to cook him. In her case it was a means of murder; her cauldron worked well enough — she demonstrated on a ram — but when it came to the cooking of Pelues she omitted to utter the necessary spell. In Irish myth a much clearer comparison is available, since at the battle of Mag Tuireadh the side led by Lugh possessed the secret of a magic well, over which spells were sung by their magicians, and into which herbs were cast. When their dead were put into the well they emerged again alive, and even fitter than before.

Brân's gift of the cauldron of rebirth works, in the story of 'Branwen', to his own destruction. He is wounded in the foot by a poisoned spear, and, dying, commands that his head should be cut off and taken to 'the White Mount' in London. There it must be buried with its face towards France; and we learn later that the effect of this (as with the buried dragons of the previous chapter) is that as long as it remains buried no harm will come to the country from across the sea.

The 'White Hill' of the story is normally taken to be Tower Hill in London, the hill of the White Tower. It is a strange fact that Brân's cult still seems to be maintained there. The name 'Brân' means 'crow' or 'raven', and the raven is therefore the god's representative. It is said of the ravens which are kept by old custom in the area of the White Tower that their presence ensures (like Gibraltar's apes) that the country will be safe from invasion.

Brân, like Beli, was originally an ancient European god, one of the most ancient, in fact, of the Celtic peoples. Known to the

Bedd Branwen, a Bronze Age burial cairn by the river Alaw, is the spot where the story tells us the broken-hearted Branwen was buried.

Romanised Gauls as Brennus, he occurs in Geoffrey of Monmouth's History as Brennius, the rival of his brother 'Belinus' for the kingship of Britain. The two eventually ruled the country between them, implying that competing cults came to terms. His wading across the Irish sea, in the Mabinogion story, and a later episode there in which he lies down to form a bridge across the river Shannon, provide us not exactly with evidence but with at least a hint that he may have been some sort of water deity.

In the story the seven survivors of the battle set out, together with Brân's severed head, on their journey to the White Mount. The head they bear with them acts as a rejuvenating, or suspending, spell: they stop and feast in Harlech for seven years without noticing that time is passing. That is nothing. A little later in the journey they stop on the island of Grassholm for eighty years, forgetting all that they had suffered, and feasting in the company of the head.

Poor Branwen had set out with them, but had not got far. Both

Ireland and Britain have been laid waste by the war, and she feels the blame for it. When they land in Anglesey, near the mouth of the river Alaw, she looks back to Ireland, and with the sadness of it all her heart breaks. 'And a four-sided grave was made, and they buried her on the bank of the Alaw.' The spot had for some time been known as 'Branwen's island' by the time, in 1813, when a tumulus was found there containing an urn with the cremated remains of a simple Bronze Age burial. Indeed the low-lying west coast of Anglesey does look towards Ireland, and sometimes just after the sun has set one can see the Wicklow Hills beyond the hump of Holyhead from the tops of rises near the Alaw. The river meanders now, small and dirty, through an unremarkable countryside, and little of the burial mound is visible.

Brân's connection with the Holy Grail might seem, on the evidence so far, a little tenuous. However one of the early Grail stories, a version known as the 'Didot' Perceval from its manuscript's provenance, names the 'Fisher King' (the occupant of Grail Castle) as Bron. This is then the naming followed by others. Brân has other connections with the Grail-keeper as well as this coincidence. There is some suggestion, in 'Branwen', that he was a god of river crossings, and the Fisher King is encountered by the hero when he reaches a river which he wishes to cross. Brân was wounded by a spear, and so, we find, was the Fisher King, and in both cases the land became an uninhabited wilderness after his wounding. Both Brân and the Grail-owner had the power of feasting their supporters indefinitely. And of course both of them owned a wonderful vessel.

If the connection is agreed — and it has been powerfully argued by an expert on the subject, R.S. Loomis — then a great deal falls into place. Among other things a North Wales setting for the Grail stories becomes very probable. A number of combining factors, which I shall now set out, identify Grail Castle as the imposing ruin Dinas Brân, above Llangollen.

The Grail-seeker, in the original stories, comes to a river, finds a man fishing, and is invited to a castle. Such a castle occurs also in an

There are few more imposing sites than the much-defended hilltop of Dinas Brân.

apparently unrelated story, part of a set of tales about a Norman outlaw (in many ways a relative of Robin Hood) called Fulk FitzWarine. Interestingly the name occurs again, since the marcher lord who owned Dinas Brân during the Norman period was John de Warenne, Earl of Surrey. Perhaps the family brought with them tales of a remote ancestor or relative, and their troubadors attached them to their local property. In any case a mid-thirteenth century French romance tells of a visit by Fulk FitzWarine to a Castle of Wonders, where things took place which no-one returns to tell of, except a lone survivor — the specification which relates this castle to that of the Holy Grail. It names the castle as 'Chastiel Brân', and since the story is set on the Welsh Marches we are left in no doubt that the castle referred to is the one on this hill above Llangollen which is still known as 'Dinas Brân', Brân's stronghold.

The name of Grail Castle in almost all the most important sources is given as 'Corbenic'. This has been variously explained, for instance as coming from the roots 'cor' and 'benoit', meaning perhaps 'holy vessel', or 'holy horn' from the legendary drinking horn (again the possession of someone called Brân) which was one of the 'Treasures of Britain' in an early list. But in one instance there occurs another, and unexplained, version of this name. When Malory mentions it first, at the start of the Grail sequence in his great Arthurian amalgamation, 'Le Morte d'Arthur', he calls in 'Corbin'. 'And so he departed, and rode till he came to the castle of Corbin'. For several chapters before the start of the search, he names consistently as 'Corbin' the castle where the Grail was kept. The anomaly can be explained: Malory was translating in these passages from a version of the French 'Prose Lancelot', and as one would expect, the otherwise unexplained word 'Corbin' is an old French word, meaning crow or raven. Thus we are back, from distant parts, to Dinas Brân.

When I was researching my book about Llangollen, 'The Story of the Dee in Wales', an objection was raised to this location of the Grail material in the Llangollen area. The Grail, it was pointed out, was traditionally located in Glastonbury, in Somerset. How could

Some parts of the fortress of Dinas Brân, a ruin from an early period, still look down over the Dee valley at Llangollen.

it be thought to be in two places, and moreover two places so far apart? It was then that yet another element appeared which makes the identification all the more compelling. There turns out to be a further coincidence relating these two places, which makes it seem probable that the Grail, or if you prefer, its stories, moved from the one to the other.

The clue (which, like so many revelations, lies right in front of our eyes) is that Glastonbury and Llangollen have something else in common, apart from having a hill above them topped by an evocative ruin. St Collen, Llangollen's founding saint and the origin of its name, was also at one time Abbot of Glastonbury. Further investigation revealed that he came to Llangollen from Glastonbury, rather than the other way round.

Collen's story is a remarkable one. The only authority we have for it exists in a sixteenth century manuscript, but it contains what appear to be early details. He was a seventh century figure, born in Ireland, brought up in Britain, educated in France. He makes his first appearance in story, however, at Southampton, where he successfully challenges a pagan to single combat, as a result of which the pagan's whole people are converted to Christianity.

Collen was, at the time, a soldier, in some versions a mercenary in the Roman army, and he did not take holy orders until he came to Glastonbury, where he landed after the episode with the pagan. Once in the church he rose fast. Only three months after becoming a monk at Glastonbury he was chosen to be Abbot. He travelled then, preaching, for three years, before returning to Glastonbury for a further five. He was, it seems, a short-tempered man, and his cursing his neighbours for their sinful lives led to his retreat as a hermit on Glastonbury Tor.

While on that magic mountain he overheard two men talking. They were talking about the king of Fairyland, the land known in Welsh as 'Annwn', the Celtic otherworld. Collen told them to stop their foolish talk. A short time later a messenger came to his cell inviting him to meet the king of Annwn. He refused, but the messenger, persistent, came back the next day — and the day after. Collen, under threat and running out of patience, eventually

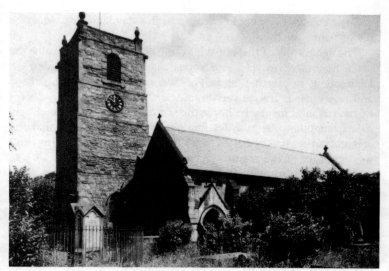

The church of Llangollen was founded by St Collen, formerly abbot of Glastonbury.

agreed to attend the meeting, which was to be on top of the Tor. He took the wise precaution of bearing a phial of holy water with him.

Sure enough on top of the hill he found a magnificent castle crowded with guards and retainers. It was all very fine, and the king on his throne welcomed him hospitably. He was offered whatever food and drink he most preferred, and gifts of all kinds. We cannot help feeling that Collen is something of a spoil-sport when he sprinkles the scene with holy water and it all disappears. Nevertheless, as I have pointed out elsewhere, the fact that he could do that, and that he came prepared, indicates a lingering belief in such an otherworld. 'You cannot sprinkle with holy water something which was never there.'

For one reason or another Collen's period at Glastonbury had to end after this adventure. He prayed for a place to go where he might live peacefully, and was instructed to travel until he came across a horse, which he would then mount. He was to ride it round as large an area as he could encompass in a day, and that would be his territory for life.

The geography of this episode is thoroughly distorted, since the place he ended up was, and appears to have been intended as, Llangollen, in North Wales. This was where he ended his days, and was buried. In one version of the story, however, he sets off eastwards, and meets the horse the same day, which would clearly rule Llangollen out as a destination. We must suppose that the original author had been to one of the places, but not the other, and was ignorant of the relation between them.

There is a story of an encounter of Collen's which takes place above Llangollen, in which he combats a giantess who is terrorising the area and in due course defeats her. He washed the blood off in a spring which is still called Ffynnon Gollen, 'Collen's well'. Until the eighteenth century an old building connected to the west of the church tower was said to house his tomb, but this seems now to have disappeared. The most interesting features in the church there now date from the early sixteenth century. There is no doubt, however, that it was at Llangollen that the saint was thought to have spent the rest of his life.

Did he then, perhaps, bring the Holy Grail with him, when he came from Glastonbury? Or, to put it more prosaicly, did the stories about the Grail follow or accompany him, for instance by being brought by his companion monks, as (it seems) did the stories about Collen himself? The Grail itself is, of course, a symbol, an image. There is no point in searching for it in the geographical world, because you can only find it in yourself, which is why the Grail-search is as much about the seeker as the Grail. There are evidently certain places, though, where such things can better be done than in others.

These ruins on the hill above the river Dee at Llangollen more than amply suit the descriptions in the early Grail stories. The Grail-seeker Peredur in the Welsh stories, Perceval in French, comes to a river, with a castle above it. The owner of the castle is fishing in the river, and there are of course few better fishing rivers than the Dee.

Dinas Brân has about it an air of emotive suggestion, very much in the way that Glastonbury Tor stands out as a physical manifestation of undefined significance. One cannot avoid the feeling of wonder when one sees it, just as one reacts with both surprise and recognition at every sight of Glastonbury Tor. Some almost overt message is conveyed by the crumbling crags of Dinas Brân's walls, in that superbly dominant position on its high, round hill. The view from it over the valley and towards the surrounding uplands also carries an otherworld aura and even the history of the place contains the right sort of elusiveness, since it has been a ruin since about 1282. Before that it was a seat of a prince of northern Powys, Madog ap Gruffudd, who reigned at the start of that century.

There is some confusion about the dates and succession of the princes of Powys Fadog, as this area of northern Powys was called, which is not at all helped by the fact that for more than a hundred years they were successively named Gruffudd ap Madog and Madog ap Gruffudd. A charter was issued from Dinas Brân in the name of one of them in the year 1270, so they still evidently ruled there then. The Normans arrived in the area in force in the year 1277, by which time the castle had been burnt, and in 1282 it was handed over, in a neglected state, together with other lands in the area, to its new Norman owner, John de Warrenne. Earl Warrenne favoured his new castle at Holt, and neglected Dinas Brân. Thus by the time the story of 'Fouke Fits Warin' (as it reads in one of its variant spellings) was written it had already been set on fire and destroyed and was probably never repaired.

Insulated from the world by its height and dominance, a thousand feet up in the air over this impressive landscape, and well protected by a massive system of ditches and ramparts, the ruined castle stands absorbed in its own air of antiquity just as it has done since the thirteenth century. The site was almost certainly an ancient place of settlement even then. It had originally been defended long before. Indeed in times of defensive compounds no-one could have neglected it. The outer ring of an Iron Age fort, and probably other associated earthworks, loops around it along a contour below the summit. Within the medieval compound may be seen the hollows of Iron Age hut circles.

Of the thirteenth century building there is still surprisingly much to be seen. Part of the wall of the Great Hall still stands, with two tall windows looking out over the Dee, and best-preserved is the passageway which originally formed the entrance. The base of a tower is identifiable mid-way down the southern wall, and the site of the keep, which it seems was the earliest part of the construction, can be identified at the eastern end. The rest of the walls flanking the hill's summit enclosed the bailey. The sheer drop on the north and west of the hill protects it adequately in these directions, but a huge ditch (from which came the stone to construct it) embraces the castle to its east and south. The size and ambition of style are still apparent. Nobody could ever have failed to be impressed.

It would tempt one into fanciful speculation, even without its direct links with myth. The contact here with the god Brân, through the name and through the 'Fulk' statement that this was a castle of wonders, combines compellingly with Brân's possession of a magic, resurrecting vessel (and with the various links, through 'Branwen' and 'Peredur' and the French stories) to give us some insight, at least, into the sources of the Grail themes. Other magic vessels, such as Ceridwen's cauldron, contribute their share of elements, but it is perhaps Brân's cauldron of rebirth that lies at the root of the main stream of the mystic vessel's development. Grail Castle, in principle, cannot be found. In its origins it is the Celtic otherworld itself, and in its later development it is a mystical, spiritual experience and therefore located within oneself. But if it has a physical representative in the geography of our real world, then it must be Dinas Brân that has the most convincing claims to be that.

Acknowledgements

The author wishes to record his gratitude to Arnold and Sim Rattenbury for sharing with him their insights into the world of the Cynfal valley, and to thank them for their time and assistance. The author also wishes to thank Mona Williams and Geraint Vaughan Jones for supplying information.

Illustrations